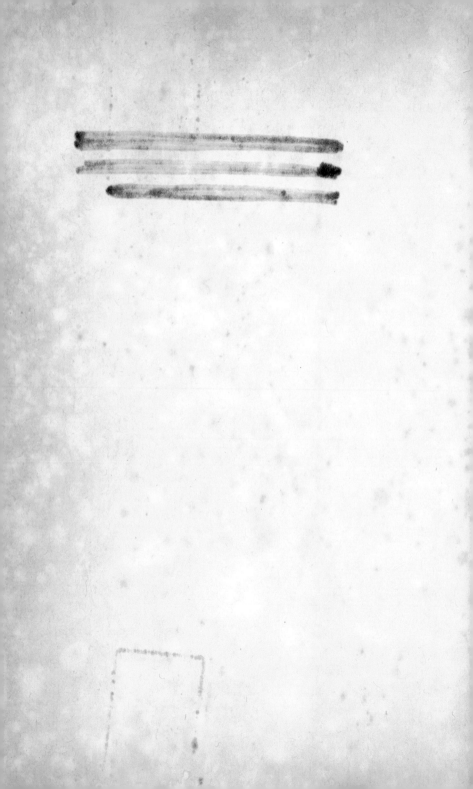

♠ ──The
Big Player

The Big Player

How a Team of Blackjack Players Made a Million Dollars

by **Ken Uston**

with **Roger Rapoport**

Holt,
Rinehart and Winston
New York

Published simultaneously in Canada by Holt, Rinehart
and Winston of Canada, Limited.

Names in this book have been changed in order to
insure privacy.

The cards depicted throughout this book are
Bicycle cards, produced by The U.S. Playing Card
Co., Cincinnati, Ohio. All trademarks registered.

Library of Congress Cataloging in Publication Data

Uston, Ken
  The big player.

  1. Blackjack (Game) 2. Gambling systems.
I. Rapoport, Roger, joint author. II. Title.
GV1295.B55U85   795.4'2   76–29919
ISBN 0–03–016921–6

First Edition

Designer: Kathy Peck
Printed in the United States of America

10 / 9 / 8 / 7 / 6 / 5 / 4 / 3 / 2 / 1

To Elsie, Senzo,
Bessie, Katie, and John
and to Erroll Garner

March 1974   Excellent health

WORK EXPERIENCE

Pacific Stock Exchange	San Francisco, Cal.
Senior Vice-President and Chief Executive Officer (Pacific Clearing Corporation)	April 1973– present
Senior Vice-President—Finance, Personnel, and Planning	November 1972– April 1973
Vice-President—Finance, Personnel, and Planning	July 1969– November 1972

American Cement Corporation	Los Angeles, Cal.
Director of Strategic Planning	December 1968– July 1969

Cresap, McCormick and Paget	San Francisco, Cal.
Senior Consultant	July 1966– December 1968

Southern New England Telephone Company	New Haven, Conn.
Director—Operations Research	February 1965– July 1966
District Commercial Manager	February 1963– February 1965
General Statistician	November 1961– February 1963
Staff Assistant— Computer Systems	September 1959– November 1961

EDUCATION

Harvard Graduate School of Business Administration MBA, Finance, 1959	September 1957– June 1959
Yale University BA, Economics, 1955, Phi Beta Kappa, Magna Cum Laude	September 1952– June 1955

All life is 6–5 against.
—*Damon Runyon*

Lᴀᴛᴇ ᴏɴᴇ ᴇᴠᴇɴɪɴɢ in January 1975 a man wearing iridescent slacks, a brown leather jacket, green patent leather shoes with three-inch heels, a diamond-studded watch, and a shiny pinky ring entered the coffee shop of the Sands Hotel in Las Vegas, Nevada, where he asked a waitress to bring him a roll. "I'm sorry," the officious woman replied, "you'll have to sit down first at the counter."

The rushed customer, who had gone without a thing to eat all day, whipped out a bill and waved it over his head crying to the waitresses, "Who'll give me a goddam roll for $20?"

Immediately a senior citizen at the counter lifted a buttered bun off his plate, swiveled around, held it out and said, "I'll sell you mine."

"No," replied the man, "I don't want to take your dinner."

A few seconds later a second waitress came over

with a fresh bun but waved off the $20 bill. The short, dark-haired man insisted she take it. "Tell that other woman," he said, pointing to the first inhospitable waitress, "that with a little courtesy she could make some tips too."

As the man stormed out of the coffee shop, patrons and the help buzzed in disbelief. They were among the latest to catch a glimpse of the most talked about gambler in town. For the past seven months thirty-nine-year-old Kenneth S. Uston (alias Ken Saunders), the senior vice-president of the Pacific Coast Stock Exchange, had been walking around the town's crowded casinos loaded down with more cash than many a Brink's truck. Because he often carried $50,000 or more at a time, the gambler was frequently chaperoned by the security guards of every club to protect him from the thieves, muggers, pickpockets, and hookers who flock to Las Vegas.

It would be an understatement to say Ken Uston bet his money recklessly. Although Vegas is a town accustomed to wildly improbable high rollers, this San Francisco executive stopped other action nearly every time he approached a blackjack pit. Fellow gamblers quit betting, dealers gave up laying out cards, pit bosses abandoned the watch on their assigned tables, bartenders ceased pouring drinks, and waitresses stopped making change as they all elbowed their way in for a better view of the unorthodox gambler.

It wasn't simply the amount Uston was putting down that attracted all this attention. After all, he wasn't the first player to spread all seven spots on the blackjack table in a $1,000-limit club with $7,000. Rather it was the flamboyant way he bet it. Running around the casino, cutting through the pit, scrambling over chairs, pushing aside customers, he put thousands of dollars into action each session. At times he seemed to be parodying small-time gamblers who played two slot machines simultaneously by actually betting blackjack tables in pairs. This peripatetic style prompted astonished pit bosses at Caesar's Palace, the MGM Grand, the Sands, the Tropicana, and other major clubs to refer to him as the Roadrunner, the Phantom, the Mad Bomber, and the Wandering Jew.

On this particular night Uston entered the nearly empty L-shaped blackjack pit at the Sands and took his unorthodox style a step further. After surveying playing conditions for a few minutes he gave two pit bosses $500 apiece with instructions to bet the money for him at nearby tables. Retiring to a seat on the adjacent casino steps, the gambler quietly finished his dinner roll while watching the first club official win $500 for him. This boss was, in turn, upstaged by the second Sands man, who won several consecutive hands for a total of $2,000. Uston walked up, collected his winnings, tipped the help, and left the casino. He had won $2,500 without even bothering to step up to a table.

Other gamblers loved this grandiose showmanship, which was quickly building Uston's reputation as one of the most daring and successful blackjack players ever to hit Las Vegas. For instance, on the night of December 14, 1974, he won $27,600 at the downtown

Fremont Hotel in forty-five minutes; early on the morning of January 5 he relieved the Holiday casino of $9,400 in half an hour; and later that month he showed up again to win $22,000 off a single four-deck shoe at the Sands.

In a town where every second person plays a system, this winning gambler appeared to be betting solely on instinct. Naturally this unscientific approach ingratiated Uston to casino managers, who were confident he would eventually take a dramatic dumping. Several clubs were willing to pick up his air fare, and Caesar's Palace offered to bring him in on their private 707, Caesar's Chariot. Hotels like the MGM Grand and the Sands vied for the privilege of letting Uston have free room and board in their $800-a-night suites equipped with white baby grand pianos, sunken tubs, mirrored ceilings, and private bars stocked with free $60 bottles of Mumm's René LaLou, Taittinger's Blanc des Blancs, and Martell Cordon Bleu. Room service provided a constant supply of hot hors d'oeuvres and assorted cold canapés. Every morning the airmail edition of the *New York Times* appeared at his door, and after his seven-course evening meal half-naked waitresses provided backrubs. Operators paged his name knowingly the way they did for Joe Louis and Telly Savalas. Security guards escorted him out to cabs. Beautiful women fought to attract his attention. And the Sands extended him that rarest of Las Vegas privileges, an A-1 player rating.

This was no small accomplishment in a community where casino owners keep one another honest by splitting up the cash take every eight hours. In fact only half a dozen players had ever qualified for this unlimited Sands rating line. Among the others was an Arab prince who generally arrived in town with $1 million in cash toted about by his armed sentries.

Uston, who generally had less than $1,000 in his personal checking account, made it onto the A-1 list by fronting for a unique blackjack syndicate. Between March 1974 and January 1975 this organization managed to show a $520,000 profit in the casinos of Nevada, Central America, the Caribbean, and France. By mid-1976, the senior vice-president and his fellow travelers would reach their goal of $1 million.

Ken Uston had originally been recruited into the enterprise in March 1974 when a professional gambler named Al Francesco phoned him at the stock exchange. "I understand you know a thing or two about blackjack," said Francesco.

"Oh, not too much, but I like the game."

"Maybe you'd be interested in playing the game?"

"Playing the game?"

"Maybe. But tell me one thing. What method have you been using?"

"Well it's been some time—but the system I was using was Thorp."

"Is that so? Well yes, you can beat the game with Thorp, but there's a lot more powerful system out now. Maybe you'd like to hear about it."

He proceeded to summarize fundamentals of the "Revere Advanced Point Count" strategy, a privately distributed blackjack counting system selling for

$200. Although Uston had never heard of this method, it sounded promising. His curiosity was especially piqued when Al added that he'd devised a method whereby one could step up the betting level a thousandfold or more in situations favorable to the player. Ken immediately asked him when they could get together.

Three days later Uston did a double take when he reached the address Al had given him in Albany, an obscure suburb on the east side of San Francisco Bay. The house looked like the kind of place a charitable realtor might list as a handyman's special. Pink stucco was flaking off the exterior, the trim appeared to be rotting away, the gutters were rusted through, one window was boarded up, and the front lawn was a mine field of dog droppings. Ken nearly tripped several times on the walkway because loose flagstone tiles kept popping out of place. At the porch he was greeted with a smirk by a couple of unshaven teenagers in dirty leather jackets who were sharing a bottle of Ripple and smoking Camels.

"Hey, Al," one of the kids yelled through the broken screen door, "there's another one here to see you."

The inside of Al Francesco's home was a surprising contrast to its exterior. The place was heavy on expensive Mediterranean furniture, gold foil wallpaper, onyx ashtrays, jade snuff bottles, crystal starfish, stoneware hippos, bronze hummingbirds, ivory elephants, black concrete poodles, and silver-plated piggy banks. A regulation cardboard and felt blackjack board was spread over the dining room table where Al, a short, swarthy man with curly black hair, was dealing cards to five players sitting on Naugahyde barstools.

Francesco asked Ken to have a seat on the living room divan until he'd finished working with the others. But as soon as Uston sat down next to an end table bearing a glass-eyed, concrete hound dog he started having second thoughts. The fact that his forty-three-year-old host looked and talked like a hit man out of the *Godfather* didn't bother him as much as the nervous expressions of the players he was dealing. He began wondering if Al's livelihood might actually be based on bilking innocents such as himself.

Certainly Uston was in no position to be investing large sums in an unproven gambling scheme. Although the exchange was paying him a $42,500 salary, much of it went toward living expenses, which included rent on a bayview penthouse apartment in San Francisco, and supporting an ex-wife. He was comfortable but certainly not affluent.

As a mathematician, computer scientist, and financial manager he'd maintained an interest in blackjack for over a decade. What got him started was a 1962 book called *Beat the Dealer* by a college mathematics professor named Edward Thorp. This landmark volume mapped out a system for counting cards that enabled the player to know scientifically when the odds were in his favor. Thorp's theory was based on the fact that the odds of the game swung back and forth between the player and the house as the cards were dealt, according to the content of the deck.* For instance, if aces and picture cards fail to show up in early hands, the player's subsequent chance of being dealt a blackjack (an ace and a ten-valued card, paying the player 3 to 2) increases. As a result, the content of the partial deck in this situation becomes more advantageous to the gambler than a full deck.† Thus when the deck is favorable the card

* This phenomenon exists because blackjack, unlike other casino games, is not subject to what statisticians call the "Law of Independent Trials." A simple example: In craps (the popular casino dice game), the odds of the player rolling a seven are 1 in 6 (there are 6 sevens on the dice out of a possible 36 combinations—6 out of 36 equates to 1 out of 6). Even if the player were to roll several sevens in a row, the chances of a seven on the next roll would still be 1 out of 6—or as professional gamblers put it, "The dice have no memory." This phenomenon also holds true for roulette, slot machines, and keno.

But blackjack isn't subject to the Law of Independent Trials because after one hand has been played, subsequent hands *are* influenced by the cards that have already been used. To take an extreme example, assume three players are playing a single-deck blackjack game. The cards are shuffled, and on the first round all three players, as well as the dealer, get a "natural" (blackjack), that is, an ace and either a picture card or a 10. On the second round, the players' chances of getting another blackjack are nil, since all four aces have been dealt. The players' advantage is clearly reduced on the second round, since the house pays 3 for 2 for blackjack, and the possibility of blackjack has been eliminated. The content of the deck is now to the players' disadvantage, as compared to the complete 52-card deck. Obviously, when the deck varies the opposite way, it benefits the player.

† There are other reasons why a deck rich in high-valued cards benefits the player in blackjack. The dealer *must* hit until he has a total of 17 or more—the player may stand with any total. Thus if the player knows there is an excess of large cards, he may stand on a poor hand, letting the dealer take the risk of drawing a large card and "busting" (exceeding a total of 21). Also, most houses offer the player "double down" and pair-splitting options, where the player may put additional money on his original bet. These options are generally more favorable to the player when the deck contains a greater than average proportion of high-valued cards. Obviously, the reverse holds true as well; when the deck is unduly replete with lower-valued cards, the odds tend to swing toward the house.

counter bets big; when it is unfavorable, he bets small. This enables the counting player to enjoy an advantage over the house.

Thorp's book became so popular that by April 1964 the Las Vegas Resort Hotel Association, alarmed by the prospect of a deluge of skilled blackjack players beating the house, announced rule changes designed to discourage counters. "In the last fifteen years there hasn't been one plane that landed without at least one person in possession of a system," explained a hotel association official. "This guy [Thorp] is the first in Las Vegas history to have a system that works."

But the vast majority of gamblers, who do not count cards, rebelled against the rule changes, and casinos were faced with the prospect of losing blackjack players. Soon the clubs went back to the old rules, assuming they could get rid of all but the most polished system players by shuffling up and barring them from future 21 play.

For several years Ken Uston had carried around his Thorp flash cards, using spare moments on planes, trains, and commuter ferries to keep the complicated system fresh in mind. As he explained to Francesco:

"The technique yielded positive results for me on Las Vegas stopovers en route home from New York business trips. Staking myself from $150 to $300, I'd play late into the evening, then catch the first morning flight back to San Francisco. Although my average win was $150 to $250, the novelty of Thorp's system wore off after half a dozen visits in 1969. I simply didn't have the $5,000 to $10,000 in discretionary funds needed to bet safely at the high levels required to generate big winnings. I knew from Thorp's book that even if one played perfectly, one could only count on earning $5 to $10 an hour at a modest betting level like mine. Since that was considerably less than what I made at the exchange, I began looking on Las Vegas as a place to unwind on my way home from the East rather than the source of a potential windfall.

"Late in 1969 I decided to stop off to hear Count Basie at the Las Vegas Sahara. Moderately drunk on Cutty Sark and water, I wobbled out of the show and elected to impress my date by casually tossing a $25 chip on the first available table. I was immediately rewarded with a blackjack. After I had beaten the dealer three more times he flipped a black $100 chip my way. I remember the awed look on the faces of the other bettors playing mostly silver. But instead of admitting that it was the first black I could ever call my own, I simply pushed it back out and won again.

"My memory of what happened after that is hazy. All I can recall is a profusion of free drinks and my date finally dragging me off to the cashier's window, where I was handed $700. When I woke up the following morning and realized what had happened I told her, 'Look, if I can win $700 drunk imagine what I can do with card counting.' We walked over to the Dunes, where Thorp failed to save me from blowing the entire $700 in an eight-hour session. That experience marked the end of my serious blackjack play."

Al laughed after Ken finished recapitulating his playing background on the night of their first meeting. "Actually the counting systems have made money for the casinos," Al told him. "Thousands of players have gone there like you with small banks. Some get wiped out because they really don't understand counting. Others don't have the money necessary to survive the swings. Another type just loses interest after finding out he's not going to make a quick killing. And then there are those who take vacation trips to Nevada where they play mostly to impress friends. The casinos start handing these guys free drinks, soon they run into some hooker who holds their hand, and before you know it they're down or out. Half the time they wake up so hung over they can't even remember which casino cleaned 'em out.

"In order to win consistently you've got to play the system instinctively, remain sober, watch for casino cheating, have a bankroll big enough to keep you going no matter how bad things get, and be willing to stick a trip out for weeks. Your win grows in proportion to the overall volume of money you put into play.

"We don't go by hunches and superstition. It's a serious business with us. We don't let people bring dates or spouses along unless they are already counting for the team. We don't drink, everyone gets plenty of sleep, and late-night partying is off limits. We don't go down there to raise hell. If there's time to kill, we spend it practicing."

Al proceeded to fill Ken in on details of the "Advanced Point Count." Although this approach appeared to be a considerable improvement on Thorp, the new recruit failed to see how it could be used effectively. "After all," he told Al, "every time you step up your bet size to take advantage of a hot deck the casino will just shuffle up on you."

"You're wrong, Ken. We've been able to win over $80,000 with this system during the past year and a half."

"How?"

"Simple. At the beginning of each session we send in a team of counters who each play separate tables and steadily bet the $2 minimum. When the deck turns highly positive they flash our team Big Player— we call him the B.P.—with a prearranged hand signal. The B.P. rushes over and puts down bets of $200 to $500 depending on the degree to which the deck favors the player. As soon as the shoe runs out or the count drops off and wipes out his advantage, the B.P. backs off to wait for the next hot deck signal from another counter. Rotating between tables manned by our players, all of whom pretend not to know him, the Big Player is able to limit his bets to positive decks."

Al went on to explain that, ironically, one casino measure designed to thwart card counters actually worked to the team's advantage. After the publication of Thorp's book many Las Vegas clubs began dealing multiple decks out of a container called a shoe. Most popular was the four-deck shoe, which made it harder to utilize Thorp's original system which was geared to a single deck.

But the advantage of four-deck over single-deck games was that the count could go up and stay high for longer periods, allowing the Revere-trained B.P. more rounds at favorable odds. In some situations it was possible to bet as many as fourteen or fifteen consecutive hands with a hot shoe. As a result the team enjoyed tremendous leverage in favorable situations. For without arousing casino suspicion they could suddenly increase their betting level at a given table from the $2 being played by the counters to $2,000 or even more put down by the Big Player. This ability to enjoy bet variations of 1,000 to 1 (and even more in some cases where the B.P. played several hands simultaneously) was what every blackjack player dreamed of. Now there was a safe way to keep bets down in unfavorable situations and immediately step them up when the deck turned positive.

It didn't take a Harvard Business School degree to appreciate the financial implications of what Al was saying.

"But why are you telling me all this?" Ken asked.

"Because I want you on the team," he explained.

"You don't even know me."

"True, but you know mathematics, you don't look like a gambler, and I'm assuming you wouldn't mind making some real money."

He was right, of course, although at the time Ken viewed participation in Al's team primarily as an adventure.

Francesco proceeded to teach him the rudiments of Advanced Revere. First they went over the values assigned to each card. The value for 5s was +4; for

4s, it was +3; 6s, 3s, and 2s were counted +2; 7s were +1; 8s were 0; 9s were −2, while 10s and face cards were −3. Aces were 0 but had to be counted separately. Using these values, Al started him going through a full deck, keeping track of the cumulative count. After they practiced awhile the leader went off to help some of the other players visiting that day. By the time he returned Uston was able to work his way through all fifty-two cards in about two minutes. "Not bad," Al said. "When you can do it in twenty-five seconds we'll let you join the team."

A sensible rationale lay behind this tough standard. The counter who couldn't go through a deck in 25 seconds probably wouldn't be able to keep track at the tables. And if he couldn't instinctively maintain the running count, there was no way he was going to be able to play each hand in accordance with the team's basic strategy, determine when the deck was hot enough to call in the B.P., give smooth signals, and handle the crucial ace-adjustment side of the job.

Since an ace-rich deck benefits the player,* these cards are accounted for separately. By knowing the number of aces left in proportion to the total number of cards remaining it is possible to determine whether the deck is ace-rich or ace-poor. This information is invaluable for betting purposes. Sitting down next to Ken and pointing at his feet, Al showed him how counters kept track of aces:

* When the deck is rich in aces the player is more likely to receive a blackjack, and his potential for splitting aces is greater. (See the Appendix for a description of the rules of blackjack and the definition of such terms as "splitting pairs," "doubling down," and "insurance.")

"The first eight aces of a four-deck game are counted on the left foot, the second eight on the right foot. The left foot is rotated clockwise for the first four aces; thus, the left foot with the toe of the shoe on the ground and the rest of the foot raised represents one ace; the foot leaning on the instep means two aces; on the heel (toe up), three aces; and on the outstep, four aces. The toe up and pointing to the left means five aces; toe up and pointing to the right, six aces; heel up and pointing to the left, seven aces; heel up and pointing to the right, eight aces. Aces nine through sixteen are done identically on the right foot, starting in a clockwise direction. Come on now, you do it."

"Is this some kind of initiation stunt?" Uston asked.

"No," Al insisted, "this is serious. Start moving."

For the first time that evening Al's five other students put down their cards to watch Ken play footsie with the teacher. When Ken finished rotating through all sixteen positions everyone applauded.

"Not bad," Al told him, "not bad at all for a senior vice-president."

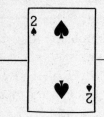

463.151 *Regulations requiring exclusion, ejection of certain persons from licensed gaming establishments: Persons included; duty of licensed establishments.*

1. The commission may by regulation provide for the establishment of a list of persons who are to be excluded or ejected from any licensed gaming establishment. This list may include any person:

    (a) Who is of notorious or unsavory reputation;

    (b) Who has been convicted of a crime which is a felony in the State of Nevada or under the laws of the United States or a crime involving moral turpitude; or

    (c) Whose presence in a licensed gaming establishment would, in the opinion of the board or commission, be inimical to the interests of the State of Nevada, or of licensed gambling or both.

—*Gaming Licensing and Control*
Nevada Revised Statutes

THE MORNING AFTER his meeting with Al, Uston arrived early at his spacious, tastefully modern office. Sitting down in his high-backed leather chair, he cast aside the *Wall Street Journal* and emptied the contents of his attaché case on the broad walnut desk: a deck of standard playing cards, Al's basic strategy chart, and the revised edition of Thorp's *Beat the Dealer*. Breaking out scissors, felt tip pens, Scotch tape, and glue, Uston began putting together a set of "basic strategy" flash cards resembling the kind third graders use to memorize multiplication tables. Abbreviated questions, such as "9, 9?" ("When do you split 9s?"), went on the front while the answers appeared on the back, such as "2–9, X 7" ("When the dealer's upcard is 2 through 9 except if it's a 7").

Uston got through only half a dozen cards before he was interrupted by a call from the vice-chairman of the exchange, who wanted a report on the Pacific Clearing Corporation, a 300-employee exchange subsidiary that Uston had taken over the year before. This unit maintained a West Coast securities depository founded in 1972 that housed millions of dollars in stock certificates for brokers across the country. But the operation was poorly conceived and run. Unfortunately, by the time Uston took over the operation it was losing $20,000 per month, had no upper or middle management, and owed $1.5 million in dividend arrearages—more than the exchange's net worth. Brokers were threatening to go to the Securities and Exchange Commission if they didn't get their dividends.

Working sixteen-hour days throughout the summer

of 1973, Uston led a new team that rescued the depository, thereby saving the entire operation from being forced into selling out to the New York Stock Exchange (which probably would have led to whole-sale transfers and/or firing part of the staff). By the fall, dividends were under control, most stock records balanced, and the exchange began showing a profit for the first time in many months. Uston was rewarded with an all-expenses-paid Hawaiian vacation.

Upon his return, however, his ninety-hour week dropped to thirty, as the exchange's new president-elect began emasculating his authority. Since all the vice-president's subordinates were now required to report directly to the top man, Uston's days were increasingly taken up with minutiae. For instance, the call this morning involved the clearing corporation's plans to rent a $600-per-month Seattle bank office to process Pacific Northwest stock certificates—Uston was always getting calls about such tiny items in his $12 million budget. He could never understand why the board would not even wink at a $2- or $3-million deal, yet devote hours worrying about the smallest detail:

"Having been subjected to this sort of petty cross-examination countless times, it was easy for me to keep up my card counting while reassuring anxious board members. As the day progressed I fielded a long series of calls about a pending report on the future of the exchange, daily financial reviews, employee recruitment, and other problems of questionable urgency. But my only clear recollection is that by five that afternoon I could count the entire deck down in twenty-five seconds. Within days my desk was filled with flashcards and other paraphernalia to help in mastering basic strategy, team signals, and ace adjustment. While continuing to authorize, report, confer, propose, reject, meet, hire, and fire, I was careful not to let my job responsibilities interfere with my new preoccupation.

"After work I attended a series of training sessions at Al's home, where he lectured with the aid of his blackboard and blackjack table. Like the other counters studying with me, I was subjected to a variety of pop quizzes, written tests, and card-playing exams timed to stopwatch accuracy. At several of these sessions I had a chance to talk with some of the team members, who helped me piece together the background of this unusual gambling operation."

The founder was a high school dropout from Cicero, Illinois, who had brought his family to California in 1960 to open a fried chicken franchise. Life went fine for the Francescos until one day Al caught his wife Julie in bed with another man whom he nearly strangled to death. His faith in monogamous relationships shattered, he got a divorce, losing custody of both his sons and half the franchise. Several years later Julie died of cancer and the boys moved in with their father. It was difficult for Al to devote the necessary attention to his sons because he was constantly out of town working on the development of four West Coast computer dating companies. Within a year Al could boast to friends that his matchmaking empire was responsible for ten marriages a week. But then he made the mistake of trying to take the enterprise nationwide. He overestimated the market, expenses soon surpassed revenues, IBM came to reclaim its computers, and the doors to his business were closed. Al was forced to turn to weekly poker games in Oakland and suburban Pleasant Hill to support himself and his sons.

Averaging about $2,500 a month from these two regular games, he had enough left over for occasional gambling trips to Las Vegas and northern Nevada. Al had been playing blackjack off and on since the publication of Thorp's *Beat the Dealer* in 1962. Although he was able to come home a few hundred dollars ahead each time, his modest betting level precluded dramatic victories. Al's biggest worry on these trips was that the casinos were cheating him.

Ironically, it was this fear that created his first difficulties in Las Vegas. In 1966 he had developed an electronic signaling device to protect against house scams. The gambler began using it with the help of his younger brother Angelo, who resembled Al so closely that many people mistook him for a twin. Whenever dealer cheating was suspected, Al's brother would push a battery-powered unit that activated a unit strapped to the gambler's leg. As soon as Al felt a buzz against his thigh he would gather up his chips and go off to find an honest dealer at another table.

Unfortunately, one day Al and his teammate were hauled in by the Riviera Hotel's security police, who confiscated the equipment, assuming it was part of some crooked scheme. Despite their protestations both men were photographed and given a place in the black book of known cheaters maintained and circulated by the Griffin Detective Agency (a firm re-tained by many Nevada casinos for protection from cheaters and counters). Al tried to hire Melvin Belli to sue over this violation of his civil rights but the famed attorney wasn't interested.

As a result Al was soon making trips to Las Vegas with a suitcase full of wigs, beards, mustaches, and makeup. Inspired by John Howard Griffin's *Black Like Me* he even began studying the possibility of developing an Afro-American disguise through liberal applications of walnut oil. But he gave up after dis-covering this technique failed when it came to touch-ing up his eyelids.

While continuing his search for better camouflage Al also kept hunting for a more effective approach to blackjack. In 1971 a friend told him about the prom-ising new system developed by Lawrence Revere. Al was soon on a plane to Las Vegas to look up Revere. He bought the private system for $200 and took several $50-an-hour lessons from its inventor. Revere, also known as Spec Parsons, had been around Las Vegas for years. Although he knew blackjack thor-oughly, he was an ineffective teacher. Impatient with his students, he would shunt them into a back room, saying, "You've got to practice more—you don't even know the fundamentals," while the $50-an-hour meter was still running.

Revere was so impressed with Al's dedication to the game, however, that he invited his new pupil on a gambling trip to Central America. Francesco nat-urally accepted the invitation. Revere, master of blackjack but not of travel regulations, assured him that no passport was necessary to get into Panama. Al met the teacher and his young girl friend (Revere was nearly sixty and had an unhealthy casino pallor, yet he was always surrounded by beautiful young women.) at the Los Angeles airport, where they learned passports were, in fact, mandatory for the trip. As a result the group changed their tickets and flew off for a short Mazatlán vacation. One of Al's clearest recollections is that Revere kept telling his girl friend to eat fruit every day so she could be as regular as he was. After returning from Mexico the two men planned another Panama trip, even though Al had developed some misgivings about playing with his guru. From their conversations in Mazatlán he suspected that Revere wouldn't be willing to bet the big money necessary to make a substantial profit. The gambling theoretician had bragged to Al that he'd made $5,000 on one trip, apparently his biggest victory ever. This didn't impress Al, who had recently been enjoying considerably larger wins in Nevada.

His fears were borne out in Panama, where their bets were limited to $50 per hand. Discouraged after several days' play, Al was getting ready to leave when both he and Revere were picked up by Panamanian police. The two gamblers spent the night in a cold cell where interrogation was complicated by the language barrier. They were released the following morning with no explanation of why they had been picked up or let go. Revere decided to head home immediately, but Al elected to stay on a few days to scout casinos and practice the new system.

Francesco returned to California convinced that Revere's system was the answer to his problems. Now the only serious worry was finding a way to vary his bets without getting caught by the bosses. During the summer of 1972 "the idea" hit him: Why not divide the counting and playing duties among several players? He pioneered the team concept by recruiting his brother Angelo plus two old poker-playing friends. One was Jon Fredrickson, a prosperous tire dealer and Englebert Humperdink look-alike; the other was Sid Mullen, a young landscape architect whose elevator shoes brought him up to five feet four inches.

But even before the team left San Francisco Al began encountering resistance to his ban on bringing nonplaying spouses or friends along for the trip. Sid had insisted on taking his wife along. To be diplomatic, Al put her to work posing as his girl friend for cover purposes. The idea was that she would hang on Al's arm, enabling him to pretend to be the typical weekend high-roller. But Sid, who was used to wearing the pants in his family, had a hard time accepting his subordinate role. To attract attention away from his wife he tore out of the downtown Union Plaza casino in the midst of a session, claiming he had been getting heat from security.

The fledgling team panicked over this fabricated incident and decided to leave immediately. Convinced that police checkpoints had already been established at the Las Vegas bus station and airport, the group rented a car and drove to Los Angeles, where they boarded a flight back to San Francisco. Scared by the experience, Al didn't schedule another trip for three months and vowed never to work with Sid again.

Al then added another poker-playing friend to his

organization, a man named Ron Reardon. This 138-pound salesman had recently lost his job as president of Black Jesus Bible Inc. It wasn't that he had proven ineffective at marketing the $39.95 edition of the King James Bible. Indeed, thanks to Ron's innovative efforts, the Black Jesus edition had found its way into tens of thousands of Afro-American homes. But just as the operation began showing a profit, religious critics began attacking the book's thesis that Jesus Christ was a black Messiah. Illustrations portraying Mary and Jesus as black—a black Jesus delivering the Sermon on the Mount, a black Jesus at the Last Supper, and a black Jesus on the cross—were dubbed frauds. When word subsequently leaked out that Black Jesus Bible Company President Ron Reardon was Caucasian, customers began demanding their money back.

"This whole thing is on the up and up," Ron swore to the suspicious customers. "Our Bible has an impeccable scholarly basis. Take Song of Solomon 1:5–6: 'I am black but comely O ye daughters of Jerusalem. Look not upon me because I am black.' What better proof could you possibly ask for?"

The customers were not impressed, and within months the president stepped down to make way for the receivers. But Ron didn't worry, for he still had his poker-playing skills to fall back on. He continued supporting his former wife, expensive apartment, and late model Eldorado convertible by playing cards. Forty-one-year-old Ron accompanied Al on several gambling trips, including a month-long journey to Central and South America. Betting $100 bills while everyone else played dollars, the pair made quite a stir. But when it came time to convert Colombian pesos back to dollars at the end of their journey, problems developed.

Because it was illegal to change large sums of foreign currency into American money, they were forced into the black market. Ron ended up in a peasant shack putting his money down in front of a young native who promptly produced a wad of American Express traveler's checks signed top and bottom. Afraid they might be stolen, he refused to accept them. Insulted, his host reached into a drawer and pulled out a magazine advertisement that showed Karl Malden testifying to the universal acceptability of the checks. But when Ron refused to waver, the young man finally handed over a batch of small American bills.

Not everyone invited to join Francesco's organization accepted initially. Tony Atkins, a poker-playing friend and Oakland attorney, initially declined Al's offer and suggested that the team might be better off taking his unemployed girl friend Judy Elliott. As with most of the women he dated, Tony met Judy when she asked him to handle her divorce. Not that there was anything unethical in this. At the age of forty-six he had handled enough cases to abide by the cardinal rule of domestic relations law: "Never sleep with a client until you've got your fee. Otherwise you may get hit for a free divorce."

Judy, who was thirty-one, had been impressed by Tony from their first meeting. The lawyer's good looks, charm, and tough-minded courtroom manner made him one of the East Bay's top dozen divorce specialists. His six-figure gross, Thunderbird, and $300 suits testified to his popularity. Hundreds of Bay Area divorcées swore by him. Judy would never forget how patient he was the first time she sat down in front of his 92-inch desk balanced on chrome pedestals. When she related how her estranged husband took their two children to the zoo with his new girl friend, Tony was outraged. "It's a terrible thing what this man has done to you. If only he were as true and loving to you and your children as I am to my family," he said, nodding toward a picture of his wife on the wall.

After Judy's divorce the pair began seeing each other at every opportunity. It was easy for Tony to meet her at a nearby hotel. Recently laid off from her job as a World Airways flight attendant, Judy had yet to find new employment. For the time being, playing blackjack seemed like a profitable way to spend her time, so when Al invited her to join the team, she gratefully accepted.

By the fall of 1973 Al had half a dozen trained counters working for him and was beginning to think about training another Big Player in addition to himself. This would enable the team to split into two groups that could play different casinos simultaneously. Initially he had Ron in mind for the promotion. But one October night he met a promising newcomer named Barry Gebhardt, a close friend of counter Jon Fredrickson, at the regular Thursday night Oakland poker game. Barry was a hip twenty-five-year-old real estate speculator with long red hair who had managed to accumulate four houses over the previous two years with no down payment. Although he'd never gone past high school, Barry, who favored silk shirts, white shoes, blue leather jackets, and double-knit pants, was a mathematical genius and had a highly optimistic and aggressive attitude about everything he undertook. He was also a remarkable poker player.

Barry had raised the $1,000 buy-in that night with cash advances on his Bank Americard and Master Charge. Unfortunately he lost the entire sum within the first fifteen minutes and was forced to ask Al to cash a $2,000 rubber check.

"The check *is* OK, isn't it?" asked the leader as he handed over the chips.

"You can count on it," said Barry looking him square in the eye as he tried to decide which house he'd have to sell to cover it. Fortunately he managed to dig out and end up $6,000 ahead for the night.

Several weeks later Al called Barry to invite him to a game in Pleasant Hill. "There's some good players but there's this one guy—a real turkey—who made some money at a game we had last Thursday. He was lucky and he's coming back for more."

"How much are we talking about?"

"No buy-in's been established, but it's a big game. I'm bringing about three grand and so is Jon."

"Count me in, man."

The turkey, Bob Wilson, proved to be exactly that. By the time the game was over, he had lost $11,000 and wrote checks for $4,000 to Al, $3,000 each to Barry and Jon, and $1,000 to the other players.

The following morning, Francesco called Barry with bad news. "I just got back from the bank. Wilson's check bounced."

"That sonofabitch. Does he have any property?"

"I think he's got a house somewhere in the East Bay. I'll look into it and come by your place this afternoon. Maybe we can figure out a way to collect our money."

At 3:00 P.M. Al arrived at Barry's house to report on his findings. "I don't think we'll collect. The house is in his wife's name, and I can't even reach him. For all I know, he skipped town."

Barry shrugged. He was even better than Al about not looking back—not thinking, "if only . . . ," or indulging in what is called "gambler's regret."

"Screw it," Barry said. "I'm going to Tahoe to play some blackjack."

"You know how to play?" asked Al.

"Hell, no. Just going up to play a few hands, fool around, find a lady, and see Isaac Hayes."

"You know, Barry, the game can be beat. In fact, I've been playin' it for years. Ever heard of Thorp's book on blackjack?"

Barry hadn't. Al went on to explain card counting and the team concept. Within an hour the young gambler dropped his weekend plans and drove back to Al's house to begin his first lesson. Although he'd never played blackjack seriously, he mastered the system in just a few sessions. The two gamblers became close friends and the new recruit even admitted to the $2,000 rubber check. "Barry," Al said after listening to the story, "you're going to fit right into this organization."

In early December Barry made his first team trip along with Al, his brother Angelo, and Ron. He was just getting his bearings at the team's first Sands session when he suddenly noticed his teammates had disappeared. Not sure of what to do, Barry headed back to the El Morocco Motel, where he discovered his roommate Ron had checked out. Reconciling himself to the fact that the whole operation had merely been a scam designed to bilk him out of the $2,000 he had put in the team bank, Barry lay down and calmly watched television for six hours.

Finally, just as Barry was about to head for the airport, Ron returned, explaining that Al and Angelo had been busted. In the back room of the Sands Angelo was accused of peeking at the dealer's hole card and flashing the information to Al via a hand signal.* Over the players' protests the Sands officials insisted on subjecting them to a full body search. After the security team had assured the management that the gamblers weren't hiding suspicious devices, they were photographed, relieved of the $2,000 Al had won during the session, and evicted. "Hope I didn't scare you by pulling out," Ron told Barry, "but I was afraid of being picked up as part of the team."

By the time Al returned to Albany he knew his Las Vegas Big Player days were over. Now assured of a permanent listing in the black book, Francesco knew

* A common method of cheating. One player stands to the rear of the dealer and reads the value of his hole card when the dealer checks to see if he has a blackjack. The reader, or "spook," then signals its value to the player at the dealer's table, who adjusts his play accordingly. Done accurately, this technique adds about 2 percent to the player's advantage.

he could no longer bet big at 21. As a result he immediately began grooming Barry as the team's new B.P.

To polish the new B.P.'s act, the founder took him down to Panama along with a $20,000 bank. As Al told it, "Barry was still practicing the numbers on the flight, but I wasn't worried. I figured someday this young genius would be as good a player as me, perhaps even better. I knew Barry wouldn't be afraid to bet big money, like Revere, Ron, or even me. I played for months before I could bet hundreds of dollars per hand without shaking."

As it turned out, Al's confidence in Barry was well-founded. In Panama Barry not only played the game flawlessly but also came up with some clever improvisations. Once, Al returned from the men's room and found Barry with bets on all seven of the table spots. The count had risen so dramatically that spreading the table was the best way to exploit the positive situation. Fortunately, the pit bosses were more than happy to let him repeat this variation.

With the casino oblivious to card counting, conditions remained favorable and the two men accumulated $54,000 in winnings in five weeks. But then the joker started edging toward the front of the shoe,* the bosses became wary, and the players decided it was time to leave Panama.

They flew to Paradise Island in the Bahamas where

* Since the joker signals that the decks will be shuffled, the further back the joker, the better for the player. Highly favorable situations for the player are more apt to occur toward the end of the shoe, when fewer unplayed cards remain.

casino conditions weren't as good as in Panama—players could double down only on hard totals of 9, 10, or 11 and were not allowed to resplit or redraw on aces. But money could still be made by the astute player. On the first day, the team dropped nearly $10,000. On the second, they recouped $2,400 before Al felt a guard tapping on his shoulder. He was led into the casino's security office, where he spotted Barry sitting in a chair. "You guys cheated us out of $2,400," screamed the decidedly mean-looking assistant casino manager.

"You got it wrong, man," Al yelled back. "We lost $7,600. Have your people check their records."

"We hate fuckers like you who try to rip off casinos. We want our money back."

When the two men refused to acquiesce, the guards were sent up to Al and Barry's room in the adjacent hotel. Rummaging through the luggage they found a meticulous set of records detailing the Panamanian win, as well as the flashcards Barry had been practicing with, Thorp's book, and other blackjack paraphernalia. The guards returned to the security office with Al's records.

"Mmmm," said one of the security men, "your IRS is going to love to see this."

After an hour's harassment, which included several threats of arrest, the four club officials offered to let Al and Barry go home in exchange for the $2,400 they had supposedly won.

Both of them declined the offer—after all, they'd lost $7,600, not won $2,400. Finally the casino manager said, "You guys sleep on it tonight and we'll discuss it in the morning. But stay the hell out of the casino. And by the way, we're putting a hold on your safe deposit box."

That posed a problem. Al and Barry had over $70,000 cash in the hotel box—their original $20,000 bank plus the Panama win. The two gamblers returned to the hotel and weighed their options late into the night, wondering about their rights in this country. Although Al had heard the rumors about fifty unsolved murders occurring in the Bahamas over the past year, he still wanted to hold firm. Barry argued that it was worth a couple of thousand to get back the seventy grand. He cited relevant experience from a Mexican bust that had brought an end to his marijuana smuggling career four years earlier. Level-headed as always, Barry had bribed a guard to spring him and not report the escape for eight hours. Then he had jumped in his car and made the 700-mile trip to the border at an average speed of slightly under 100 miles per hour. "If I hadn't paid off, I'd still be down there fighting off guards trying to gang bang me," he told his mentor. "Why worry about two grand if we can get back the Panama win?"

Al refused to knuckle under. A $2,400 bribe was unthinkable for the B.P. who once marched out of a motel room in his bathrobe demanding a 25¢ refund for a Magic Fingers unit that had failed to activate during a romantic interlude. Barry compromised by heading downstairs at 4:00 A.M. (after the four officials had turned in for the night), and slipping a few dollars to a cleaning woman who promptly handed over the safe deposit box. Within minutes after reclaiming their $70,000 the men caught a cab to the airport where they boarded the first plane out. Al literally kissed the jetway when they disembarked in Miami.

On the flight home to California, Barry made Al assure him that nothing like this would occur in Las Vegas should he be unmasked as team B.P. "Relax," insisted Al as he opened a screwtop burgundy tenth to let it breathe during the movie, "the worst that can happen is that you'll get thrown out of a casino like I was at the Sands."

"No jail?"

"Of course not," he laughed, "Las Vegas is the safest gambling city in the world."

463.151 Regulations requiring exclusion, ejection of certain persons from licensed establishments: Persons included; duty of licensed establishments.

3. Any list compiled by the board or commission of persons to be excluded or ejected shall not be deemed an all-inclusive list, and licensed gaming establishments have a duty to keep from their premises persons known to them to be inimical to the interests of the State of Nevada, or of licensed gambling or both.

—*Gaming Licensing and Control*
Nevada Revised Statutes

A WEEK AFTER RETURNING from the Bahamas, Al summoned Barry and Ron to an Albany conference, where he announced that Barry would take over as Big Player on an upcoming team trip to Las Vegas. Ron was furious that his old friend would pass him over for this relatively inexperienced gambler. "I've been putting in a lot of time while you guys were gone and I know all the numbers."

"Ron," Al said, "I think Barry should be the B.P. first time out. He got a lot of experience in Panama. personally winning $27,000."

"Well, I think I know the game pretty well."

"It's not like you'll never be Big Player. Barry and I are planning a trip to France next month and we'll need a B.P. while we're gone. Also I've got some expansion plans, which I'll tell you about once we resolve this trip."

With Ron placated somewhat the three men began working out the playing bank for the forthcoming session. Al and Barry would each put up 30 percent of the $20,000 bank, or $6,000 apiece. In return they would be entitled to 30 percent of the team's win or loss. The three counters would invest the remaining 40 percent at $2,667 apiece. As soon as this business was out of the way, Al revealed his long-range master plan.

"You remember in Thorp's book where he says that two players can combine their bank and make four times as much by both playing? * Well, I've got an idea that will make us more money and, at the same time, fake out the bosses even more. We'll go with two B.P.'s and seven or eight counters. We can have a bigger bank, maybe $50,000, bet more, and have two B.P.'s hitting them at the same time in two different clubs. Our earnings will quadruple. But, better yet, we can rotate the counters. On one day,

---

* Actually, Thorp showed mathematically that two players working off a $2,000 bank would earn four times as much as one player working off a $1,000 bank. The earnings enhancement continues geometrically as the number of players increases.

we'll have counter team A with one of the B.P.'s; the next day, we'll have counter team B with the same Big Player. The bosses will never put it together."

Ron loved this idea, since it was clear he was destined to become the second B.P. After the meeting broke up Al turned to some of his many other administrative obligations. Now that he had freed himself from playing responsibilities, he had the time to tend to the dozens of little problems cropping up in the burgeoning operation. He was a kind of combination godfather, chief executive officer, coach, banker, personnel manager, travel agent, and chef for the team; he calculated the playing bank and determined betting levels, raised shares from counters who had money, loaned funds to those who didn't, reserved everyone's flight on a group discount basis, and established a combination command post–field kitchen at the Las Vegas apartment of his girl friend K. P. Carey, a beautiful, green-eyed, twenty-six-year-old cocktail waitress. At first he had kept her in the dark about the group, claiming to be in the real estate business. But she got curious after waking up one morning to find a thick roll of $100 bills peeking out from under Al's pillow. After the leader filled her in on the operation she insisted on being taught how to count and eventually became a team member.

When Ken joined the group in the spring of 1974, Al was in the midst of a major expansion. Because team profit levels increased as the group put larger sums into play, more counters were being added every trip. The leader was spending a considerable amount of time hunting for new talent, usually picking nonprofessional gamblers who would help protect the team cover. He had been anxious to get Uston going because of the vacancy left by Jon Fredrickson, who had left the group for religious reasons. Jon's decision had come as a shock to everyone in the organization. He first broke the news to Barry at an East Bay restaurant in Concord. The new B.P. had suggested the meeting to talk over ways of collecting on the $11,000 worth of rubber checks that Wilson had written during the big poker game the previous fall. But Jon wasn't concerned. "I'm not going to worry about my $3,000," he explained, "it will come to me if the Lord wants me to have it."

Politely trying to change the subject, Barry picked up the dice sitting on the bar and said, "Come on, Jon, I'll shake you to a drink."

"I'm sorry," replied the tire merchant, "but I've stopped shaking and I've stopped drinking."

"Well I'll be goddammed," said Barry.

"And I'm not swearing anymore either."

Over a brief lunch Jon explained that he had decided to forsake gambling life for the Jehovah's Witnesses. As they were leaving, he reached into his briefcase and handed Barry a copy of the latest *Watchtower* magazine, explaining, "If you really want to understand what's happened to me just read this."

Jon subsequently visited the homes of several other players, trying to interest them in his newly adopted religion. Despite a cool reception, he retreated gracefully. Walking out the door of Al's house one Saturday morning he said quietly, "You may all think you're getting away with something in Nevada.

But I hope you'll remember one thing. There is no place you can hide from the Lord. No place."

Although they all laughed off Jon's admonition at the time, they certainly realized that by merely stepping into a casino they were subjecting themselves to total surveillance. In Vegas it isn't enough simply to have guards and plainclothesmen watch for player cheating and theft—in this ultimate police state private security forces hang from the rafters on the other side of the one-way-mirrored ceilings keeping an eye on the pit bosses, dealers, guards, and plainclothesmen. It's a town where even Big Brother has someone looking over his shoulder.

In a way these precautions make some sense. Ken knew that in Vegas people don't conduct their business as they do at Southern New England Telephone or the Pacific Stock Exchange. In this city broken promises, meaningless handshakes, and unenforceable agreements are a way of life; taking out a contract doesn't mean beginning a business relationship—it means terminating it.

Given this moral climate, it's understandable that the new recruits were jumpy at first about their leader's determination to conduct business on the basis of good faith and a handshake. As professionals who drew people into overinsuring, buying dubious stocks in a bear market, grabbing houses situated on earthquake faults, and taking home used cars with turned odometers, they had plenty of reasons to be cynical about any business transaction. Even Uston, in all his years with the phone company, Cresap, McCormick and Paget (one of America's leading management consulting firms), American Cement, and the exchange, had never run into anyone quite like Al. But it didn't take him long to discover that an oral agreement with Francesco was worth more than any legal document he'd ever signed.

Al always kept his word, which may have been why he became so vindictive when others failed to keep theirs. For instance, one time Francesco's fourteen-year-old son took $1,300 worth of his father's gambling winnings that had been stashed at home. After discovering what had happened, he didn't hit the boy, cut off his allowance, or sit him down for a man-to-man talk; he simply called the police. Al dropped charges against his son several days later after he agreed to return the stolen money. This incident prompted many of the players to begin taking precautions with the large sums they carried around. Counters began traveling to Nevada with thousands stuffed in their shoes, socks, bras, and pantyhose. Al stressed the importance of this and other team safeguards (such as not leaving any gambling paraphernalia in hotel rooms) to the counters during their early training sessions. Even in San Francisco, Uston made a point of locking his office door whenever he began one of his increasingly frequent practice sessions, for by this time he was anxious to pass all the team tests:

"I practiced continually to memorize the call-in numbers used by counters when they brought in the B.P. to play a hot deck. Under this system the minimum count required to justify calling in the Big Player varied with the number of decks in the discard pile. For instance, if one deck had been dealt from a four-deck shoe, the count (adjusted for the number of aces played) had to be at least +24 before the Big Player could be brought in. This way he was assured of starting play at a minimum 1 percent advantage over the house. [Odds for these and all other situations had been confirmed through computer runs.]

"Each counter kept the Big Player posted on his or her deck's status through a set of prearranged signals. This sign language, also used for general intrateam communication, was the group's way of keeping in touch without exposing the operation. Another illustration of Al's ability to out-think casino security, these signals were all common bits of body language that would not attract a second glance from anyone outside the team.

"Thus, when a counter innocuously dropped his hands in his lap, he was actually notifying the B.P. that the deck was seriously to the team's disadvantage. Hands on the table rim meant the deck was average. As the count approached the call-in number, the counter flashed the warm-deck sign by placing his hand on his cheek. And as soon as the call-in number was reached or exceeded, he flashed the hot signal by holding his head in his hands.

"When the B.P. arrived at the table, the counter used a set of arm signals to supply the current running count. This all-important number permitted the Big Player to make the correct playing and betting decisions. If the count was sky high, he would bet more, double down, and split pairs more frequently. As the count dropped off he would begain playing more conservatively, finally leaving when the deck was no longer favorable.

"Some of the counter's responsibilities, such as mastering call-in-number arm signals, could be practiced while driving about town in my Sprite. Under this system, tens were signaled by the *placement* of the right hand on the left arm (for example, hand on biceps was +40), while units were shown by *motions* of the right hand (for example, rubbing forefinger and middle finger of the right hand up and down the left hand indicated a 3). Thus, to signal +43, a counter grabbed his bicep and then rubbed his right-hand fingers up and down his left arm.

"En route to Monterey one weekend for the annual Pacific Stock Exchange outing, I devoted the entire three-hour drive to practicing these arm signals. With my left hand on the steering wheel, my right was free to indicate various numbers read off license plates. By the time I reached the Del Monte Lodge, the sight of any two-digit license number between ten and fifty-nine (the maximum count for which there was a signal) instinctively led me to touch my left arm, flashing the appropriate signal.

"After checking in at the hotel, which overlooked the Pebble Beach golf course, I headed for the sitting room to deal blackjack, as I'd done for the past five outings. Inexplicably, the exchange's floor personnel had always let me keep the deal for the entire weekend, despite their knowledge of the house's edge. But this time, after I'd won about $200, a Los Angeles trading specialist named Sy Leopold asked, 'Hey, how come I can't have the deal?' I had no choice but to let him take over. However, with the help of the Revere Advanced Point Count Al had just taught me, I took Sy for about $300 in a three-hour session. This Advanced Point Count system was beginning to look promising."

After helping Uston for several weeks, Francesco took off on an extended gambling trip to France. During his absence Ken continued training with Ron Reardon, who was destined to become the team's second Big Player. Studying with him was another aspiring counter named Mike Barker, who had done saleswork for Ron's defunct Bible-publishing empire. Although the sixty-two-year-old counter had played Thorp in Nevada for over ten years, he had a difficult time mastering the team approach. An unscientific gambler with a weakness for craps, Barker had been in and out of sales jobs all his life. He had, among other things, sold used cars, Fuller Brushes, Shaklee soap, freezer beef, linoleum, phone-answering equipment, and vinyl tops—all with little success. Fortunately, his wife Ellen managed to keep up with living expenses with her bookkeeping job at Outerspace Waterbeds.

Barker generally could win a few hundred dollars per trip at the blackjack table using Thorp. The hardest part of his sessions was getting out the door without blowing his take at the craps table. At times he would go to considerable lengths to conserve a win. For instance, late on the final afternoon of a charter trip to Las Vegas a few years back, Barker was $900 ahead in blackjack when he felt the urge to shoot craps. He quickly cleaned out his pockets, gave all the

money to Ellen, and told her to go wait in the ladies'
lounge until the bus for the airport arrived. She had to
stay there for two hours to keep him from getting his
hands on the cash and gambling it away.

After Uston and Barker had counted down decks in
twenty-five seconds, showed their understanding of
ace adjustment, given the correct call-in numbers,
flashed the right signals at the appropriate times, and
passed the fill-in-the-blank tests, Ron took them to
Reno on a weekend training trip. Unfortunately Tony
Atkins, who had also been scheduled to go along,
was forced to back out at the last moment. Having left
his wife to move in with Judy Elliott, the divorce
lawyer was now tied up with his own divorce. To set
the proper moral tone for his legal proceedings, he
had retained an attorney who also happened to be an
ordained minister. And on the Saturday of the training trip he and his lawyer were having a long
strategy session on how to play things in court.

Most of the trip to Nevada was devoted to rehearsing sign language. While Ron sped around traffic
on Interstate 80, Uston and Barker went through the
motions. "Ken, what's this?" Ron asked, stroking his
forehead with his thumb and forefinger, as they drove
through Vallejo.

"You understand a previous signal given by another
player."

"Right. Mike, what's this mean?" he asked, as he
rubbed his forefinger against his eye.

"You want the count over again."

"The aces too, Mike. You've got to repeat them
both."

"Ken, how about when I grab my crotch?"

"Meet me in the men's room."

Like animals, they scratched, rubbed, grasped, and tapped themselves all the way to Vacaville, where Ron grilled them on basic strategy.

"Ten against a 9."

"Double," they responded.

"Threes against a 7."

"Split."

By Sacramento, Ron was briefly flashing groups of five randomly selected cards to help them practice the count. Then they turned to counting down entire decks. Mike did the job in thirty seconds, while Ken pulled it off in twenty-six. "That's fair," said the leader as he proceeded to do the same thing in twenty-one seconds while driving through heavy traffic. "You'll get the hang of it after a while."

By the time they crested Donner Pass the counters had their signals down pat. They knew that the B.P. would rub his nose if he was anxious for a counter to change to a different table because a new deck was about to break or a dealer was suspected of cheating. Since it was sometimes difficult for a counter to watch his leader discreetly while working the same table, this message could also be flashed by merely tapping chips on the table. When the Big Player wanted his teammates to change to another blackjack pit he'd grasp his neck with the thumb on one side and fingers on the other. If security became a serious problem or crowded tables hurt playing conditions, the Big Player could shift the team to a prearranged backup casino by rubbing his ear.

As the Cadillac descended the eastern slope of the

Sierras, Ron pointed to the high-rise Reno casinos looming in the distance—Harrah's, Harold's Club, Jesse Beck's Riverside, and the El Dorado. "There's the enemy," he announced melodramatically. A favorite of the nickel-and-dime tour bus set from the Bay Area, Reno was certainly no match for Las Vegas, where four-deck clubs and better rules benefited the team concept. But while Al generally avoided taking the team to the single-deck clubs of northern Nevada, they made an excellent classroom for his trainees— B.P.'s could break in new players while avoiding overexposure in Las Vegas casinos.

Acting like a latter-day Peter Graves out of "Mission Impossible," Ron pulled off onto a side road just outside of town, where he hid all the team's playing decks, flash cards, tests, charts, and other gambling paraphernalia in the spare tire well. Then, as the team took the elevator up to their rooms at the Arlington Plaza, he made Ken and Mike detach their keys from the plastic identification tags explaining, "If you get searched, they won't know where you're staying."

In his room he showed everyone the team's secret door knock—two raps, a pause, and a third rap—to be used at all times. And finally he left several of the many second-rate 21 books (pushing such fallacies as never double down on a 9, never split 10s, and always insure a blackjack) atop his dresser. That way any suspicious casino employee who did search his quarters would logically conclude he was an amateur.

Several hours later, after everyone had taken the mandatory two-hour nap, they headed for Harold's Club to stage a variation of the team concept. Ron, dressed in a ratty wool shirt, took his position at a table, where he bet $1 bills while keeping track of the count. A few minutes later Ken and Mike, acting like old friends, moved in alongside their leader and started betting $5. Although they pretended not to know Ron, they stepped their bets up to $50 and $100 whenever he flashed hot or superhot signals. Because Ron was relaying all the major playing decisions through prearranged hand signals, his two companions were free to drink, kid the dealers, and purposely ignore the other players' cards to reassure the pit bosses they weren't counting. For additional cover they would try to disarm the dealer by prefacing every big bet with weak jokes like: "Hey, Mike, let's try some of these counterfeit 50s over here."

While Barker and Uston entered the clubs together, Ron was careful to always show up ahead of them and leave fifteen minutes after they were done. Ken feigned ignorance by asking the dealer if shuffling the deck was truly to the player's advantage, and Mike occupied the security guards by dropping $5 chips in front of them.

After following their leader through Harold's Club, the El Dorado, and Jesse Beck's Riverside, the players returned to Ron's room. Although they had won $750, Ron was furious. "You amnesiacs cost us $400. I flashed the superhot signal eight times. You were supposed to bet $100, not $50. And Barker, goddammit, how the hell can I call your plays if I can't see your cards? Get your goddamm hands out of the way."

"What do you mean?" yelled Mike. "I showed you my cards every time. Hell, I held them as high as I dared."

"Well, I couldn't see them. If you can't start doing it right, you should take up bridge."

Ron was even more caustic after the team's second and final night of play in Reno, when they pushed the team win up to a total of $875. Although this was a good beginning for neophytes, the teacher kept going on and on about their mistakes. Ken and Mike calmed him down over dinner. After taking in a lounge show, a moderately smashed Uston talked the group into heading to the Mustang Ranch, a bordello located on the Truckee River fifteen minutes outside of town. When the cab driver stopped in front of a ramshackle collection of trailers, Barker lost his nerve. "Listen, guys, you go ahead; I don't think this is for me."

"Come on," said Ron, "we're in Nevada. Gambling and whore houses are legal."

"I know that but I just can't cheat on my wife now after thirty-five years. It just wouldn't be right."

While the cab took Barker back to Reno, Ron and Ken rang the buzzer several times. Finally a heavy woman dressed in a pink mumu escorted the two gamblers through a barbed wire fence into a dilapidated parlor where red lightbulbs illuminated red wallpaper, threadbare carpets, old couches, and a jukebox playing Beatles music, heavy on the sitars. Half a dozen men were sitting around sipping drinks but there wasn't a single hooker in sight. The friendly hostess apologized, explaining that the entire staff was tied up taking care of a special delegation of foreign doctors.

"Doctors?" Uston asked.

"Well, actually, they aren't all full-fledged M.D.'s," she explained. "Some of them are osteopaths."

"Where's Joe Conforte?" asked Ron, anxious to meet the legendary prince of Nevada prostitution who owned and operated the Mustang Ranch as well as four other bordellos in a nearby county.

"He's taking a nap," said the hostess. "He'll be up in about an hour. You know, that man is just incredible. He just may be the most generous person in Nevada. Every year he gives away hundreds of thousands of dollars to service clubs, the little leagues, churches, school recreation programs, you name it. There are a lot of charitable organizations that would be out of business if it weren't for him. And yet the politicians are always giving him a hard time about his license."

As Ron and Ken chatted with the hostess in the drafty parlor, women dressed in gold lamé hotpants, bikinis, evening gowns, or tights and leotards gradually came out and formed a semicircle. After Ron made his choice, Uston picked out a young blond who led him through the employees' lounge, where off-duty girls were reading Agatha Christie paperbacks and munching fruit beneath a sign that read: NO FIGHTING! BOTH GIRLS REGARDLESS OF RIGHT OR WRONG WILL BE FIRED ON THE SPOT.

Turning down a long hallway illuminated by a single bare lightbulb they entered a tiny room full of teddy bears and the collected works of Khalil Gibran. As soon as the woman closed the door the outraged voice of a customer in an adjacent unit came booming through the wall: "I know that, but I'm just not leaving before I get my bubblebath."

Pretending to ignore the remark, Uston's choice got right down to business. "Well, honey. What do you want?" Embarrassed, he was unable to find the right combination of words. Finally she broke the ice: "A suck and fuck is $20."

After taking the money out to the cash register she returned and they undressed. "Bet you picked me because I look like the girl next door," she told him as they climbed onto her bed. "That's what most men tell me. All of us tend to attract a particular type. Take Jane, for example, the girl who was standing next to me. Most guys pick her because she has big boobs. Of course she's only here until she can save enough money to be a dental hygienist. She can have it as far as I'm concerned. I used to be a nurse in L.A. and after being at the Mustang for a few months I don't think I could ever go back to the nine-to-five routine. Nursing's such a bitch. Every time you turn around some man is pushing you around. And patients are dying on you all the time. Do you know that only two customers have passed away here since the place opened nineteen years ago? And they were both senior citizens."

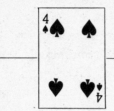

463.154 *Regulations requiring exclusion, ejection of certain persons from licensed gaming establishments: Penalties for failure to exclude, eject.*

> The commission may revoke, limit, condition, suspend or fine the licensed gaming establishment or individual licensee, in accordance with the laws of the State of Nevada and the regulations of the commission, if such licensed gaming establishment or any individual licensee fails to exclude or eject from the premises of any licensed gaming establishment any persons to be excluded or ejected.
>
> —*Gaming Licensing and Control*
> *Nevada Revised Statutes*

"TAKE THAT CANDLE AWAY!" screamed Al Francesco as he tried wrestling the expensive bottle of Clos de Vougeot away from the waiter. After just a week in Dieppe, a town on the English channel, he had worn out his welcome at nearly every good restaurant. While disputing Al's knowledge of blackjack was dangerous, contesting his views on food and drink was suicidal.

This particular confrontation started after the waiter brought out the dry red burgundy and held a lit candle under the bottleneck as he poured the wine into a Baccarat crystal decanter. Only after the bilingual maître d' rushed over to explain that candlelight was merely being used to detect sediment and keep it from escaping into the decanter did Al loosen his grip.

Part of Al's problem in Dieppe's restaurants was the language barrier. Although he was still a long way from mastering English, he insisted on trying his hand at French with consistently disastrous results. Too vain to point to the menu, Al managed to embarrass himself every time he sat down to eat. Typically, in one restaurant he ordered coffee, followed by strawberries and an omelette.

"I will bring you an omelette, then coffee and strawberries," replied the waiter.

"No," insisted Al, "first I want coffee, then strawberries and an omelette."

"You are in France," shouted the waiter. "You are not in New York. You will eat it the way I serve it."

But Francesco's restaurant problems were minor compared with the trouble he and Barry were experiencing at Dieppe's only casino. After surveying the French gambling landscape they had settled on this little club because of rules unusually favorable to the player. Besides allowing doubling down on split pairs, the dealers placed the joker four to five cards from the bottom of the shoe.

The club's tall, distinguished owner had introduced blackjack to France after studying operations at the Las Vegas Stardust in the mid-sixties. Since he knew the single-deck game could be beaten by card counters, he installed six-deck shoes at all three of his blackjack tables—a practice subsequently followed by every French casino. He hadn't been back to Nevada for nearly a decade, however, and didn't realize that Revere, Hi Opt, and other sophisticated systems now enabled counters like Al to beat multideck games.

The American gamblers, anxious to make a quick killing, began betting too high relative to their $30,000 bank. At home Al protected the team from falling into this all too common trap by calculating a conservative betting strategy before each trip. Generally, Big Players were not allowed to bet more than 1/150 of their total playing bank on any given hand because, even with a superhot deck yielding a 10-percent advantage over the house, players can take only fifty-five out of a hundred hands. In the long run this obviously works to the player's advantage, but in the short run it can tempt him to bet too high.

And that was precisely the mistake Al and Barry made in Dieppe. The casino owner watched gleefully from the sidelines as the two players proceeded to bury themselves to the point where they couldn't pay their hotel bill. Al wired his brother Angelo to withdraw the entire $17,000 on deposit in their joint savings account. Then he placed a transatlantic call to Barry's girl friend Karen Lombardi, who had recently jointed the team as a counter.

Certainly the best-looking woman in the group, Karen was expected to be terrific at taking dealer and pit boss attention away from the B.P. Although she made only a modest living as a model, her generous father, a multimillionaire Georgia auto dealer, sent her enough money to enable her to contribute a full counter's share to the team bank. In fact, at the time of the trip her cash reserves exceeded Al's. The leader instructed Karen to pick up his $17,000 from Angelo and fly the money over along with his Las Vegas girl friend, K. P. Carey.

The two couriers spent most of their polar flight practicing the count. But by the time they reached Dieppe neither was ready to go. "Al," K.P. confessed as soon as they were alone in their hotel room, "Karen and I still can't handle ace adjustment."

In the casino the women proved so inadequate that the group was forced to scuttle the original game plan, which called for Barry, Karen, and K.P. to each count one of three tables while Al roved about as B.P. After Al's girl friend made the mistake of calling him in on a minus deck, the group adjourned and decided to protect themselves by putting Karen and K.P. at the same table.

Still confused, the two apprentices periodically held up play to determine whether or not the count was high enough to bring Al in. Frequently they became so lost that they asked each other how many decks had been played, the number of aces left, and even whether the count was plus or minus. This sort of talk could have destroyed the entire effort were it not for the fact that none of the dealers spoke English. Only when the bilingual owner arrived on the scene did the women revert to a secret code, referring to aces as "Andy," plus count as "Papa," and minus count as "Mama."

Of course the Dieppe entrepreneur paid no attention to these two talkative women who were betting at the $5 level. He was far more concerned with Al, who frequently spread to as much as seven hands of 2,500 francs ($500 each). When the leader proceeded to dump $10,000 of the $17,000 worth of traveler's checks brought over by Karen, the owner began planning how he would spend this sudden windfall. He would occasionally tease Al about the ways he intended to use the house winnings. Part of it would pay for renovations on a nineteenth-century farm house he had just purchased. Then perhaps he would take his wife back to Las Vegas. He was anxious to see the new MGM Grand and she adored Wayne Newton. And, of course, now he'd have the capital required by the French government to open a badly needed fourth blackjack table.

But as soon as the owner finished making plans to hire contractors, call his travel agent, and order the new equipment, Al's luck turned. In four days he won back the $40,000 that had been lost, and three days later the group called off their stay in Dieppe $23,000 ahead. Anxious for another chance to wipe them out, the owner congratulated Francesco on his dramatic comeback and invited him to return again. "We may not have Totie Fields," he told his guest while escorting him out of the casino, "but I think you will agree that our rules are very good." Then he phoned his wife to break the bad news about Wayne Newton.

By the time the four victorious players returned from France in late May, Ron had succeeded in turning Ken, Mike, and Tony into competent counters. After the Reno trip a series of classroom exercises culminated in a Las Vegas graduation exercise during which the group won $7,000. Although this was certainly a respectable performance, Ron, who had been serving as mini-B.P., for the trip, purposely downgraded his pupils' achievements with caustic comments about their foolish mistakes. His harshest criticism was reserved for Uston, who managed to miss a key midnight session at the Union Plaza.

Actually, Ken had arrived at the downtown hotel several hours ahead of starting time with only the best of intentions. Unfortunately his ambitious plan of surveying pit conditions collapsed when he decided to rest his feet in the cocktail lounge. Within fifteen minutes he was violating the team ban on presession drinking and soon after he was pouring out his life story to Jean, a thin, dark-haired woman dressed in lemon shorts, a matching halter top, and high heels.

The narrative began in New Haven, where he had been raised with his two sisters in a $40-a-month government housing project. His father, an instructor at Yale, took home $250 per month, which barely covered the rent, food, clothes, and payments on a balky 1951 Kaiser-Frazer that was usually in the shop. A serious student, Ken had graduated from high school at sixteen and won a full scholarship to Yale, where he felt very insecure in the company of his affluent roommates. While they traveled off to Smith and Wellesley on weekends, Uston usually ended up at the local Davenport Avenue Roller Rink with old high school girl friends whom he would have been embarrassed to bring to Yale social functions.

But finally, in his senior year, his confidence bolstered by his being elected to Phi Beta Kappa, he began playing bridge in Yale's Berkeley College lounge after dinner, affected an English accent, and headed out to Smith, Vassar, and Bennington in a new J. Press suit. When Uston finished Yale he won another scholarship to Harvard Business School, marrying shortly after graduation and subsequently settling in New Haven, where he quickly became the fastest rising young executive in the Southern New England Telephone Company.

By the time he was twenty-eight, Ken rose to District Commercial Manager responsible for community relations activities in the thirty-three towns embraced by the New London District. In addition to heavy administrative responsibilities, he spent a considerable amount of time visiting branch offices, where he boosted morale by pinning anniversary buttons on service representatives and attending employee retirement lunches. At the suggestion of his employer, Uston also spent many of his nights and weekends serving on the Chamber of Commerce, YMCA, Rotary Club, and United Fund boards.

Two years later the young phone executive was promoted to director of operations research, where he directed a $200,000 study that showed that the company could save millions by centralizing business offices. But this conclusion didn't go over well with A. T. & T. officials in New York, who felt their multitude of branch offices served a valuable public relations function. As a result the document was never distributed to phone company marketing people around the country. Uston, who had expected another promotion by now, grew impatient with the progress of his career. Although he was three levels ahead of most company executives his age, Ken decided to leave the Bell System to join one of the nation's leading management consulting firms, Cresap, McCormick and Paget, in San Francisco. There he bought a bayside house in Tiburon but saw little of it due to a heavy travel schedule. By July 1969, when Uston moved up to the senior vice-presidency of the Pacific Stock Exchange, his marriage had broken up and he had moved to a penthouse apartment across the water in San Francisco.

Jean, who looked eighteen but was actually twenty-five, nodded knowingly as Ken traced his life history. Little of it surprised her. Indeed, his story bore so many similarities to the careers of her other customers that she could almost fill in the blanks. For some reason she always seemed to attract the kind of man who had worked his way up in business only to find life boring at the top executive level.

Just when Jean thought the monologue was never going to end, Ken surprised her by asking how she had come to Las Vegas. Flattered by his interest, she proceeded to tell of a conventional middle-class upbringing in Denver, disrupted at age eight by an incestuous father. "Now don't you ever let anyone do this to you," Jean's drunken dad had said as he climbed into her bed and started fondling her for the first time. His forays into the child's bedroom continued for five years, practically condoned by her mother, who thought the perverse relationship might save a rocky marriage. Finally, when Jean's grandfather started trying the same thing, she put an end to all the molestation by padlocking her bedroom door.

Soon after locking her father out the thirteen-year-old fell in love with a high school friend; he fathered her first out-of-wedlock child, who was immediately put up for adoption. At sixteen Jean dropped out of high school and married a young man, undeterred by the fact that she was pregnant with someone else's child. Divorced two weeks before her seventeenth birthday, she moved with her baby to San Francisco to get work as a prostitute. Initially unable to find babysitters willing to work odd hours, she was forced to bring customers home, only to have the child wake up and disrupt business in the middle of the night. Gradually, however, she began attracting affluent customers who could be scheduled during working hours, while the child was at a day-care center. Business went along fine for almost six years until a friend convinced Jean she could easily double her income in Las Vegas. The friend was right.

Ken suggested they might be able to do some business. Jean agreed and soon they were heading back to his room at the El Morocco Motel. He wanted to languish in bed afterward but she was in a hurry. "I've got to pick my kid up in fifteen minutes at the MGM nursery," she explained while throwing her clothes back on. "They close at midnight."

Realizing he was now two hours overdue for the Union Plaza session, Uston jumped up and rushed back to the hotel. He was too late. Well before Ken arrived Ron had already given the chest signal and sent the rest of the team off to bed. At a Sambo's breakfast meeting the following morning the trip leader chewed him out liberally, reaching his conclusion just as the waitress arrived with their blueberry pancakes. "You know what the trouble with you is, Uston? You've got a goiter for a cerebrum."

Ken made no reply. He sat there eating, thinking about his 300 subordinates back at the Pacific Stock Exchange who answered his phone, opened his mail, made his coffee, took his dictation, wrote his letters, issued his memos, mimeographed his reports, reserved his luncheon table, and, of course, carried out his executive orders. Now he was just an underling forced to take gratuitous insults from an unsuccessful Black Jesus Bible salesman whom he had entrusted with $2,000 of his own money. At first Uston had felt dubious about contributing this sum to the $20,000 team bank. After all, there was no real way of knowing whether Ron might skim some of it off for himself by pocketing a handful of $100 chips (which could be easily cashed in without the team's knowledge). Or what if he happened to go out for cigarettes and never returned? Two thousand dollars was half a year's rent.

Still, after playing with the team in Las Vegas he felt reassured. Why would Ron want to run the risk of ripping off the group that was going to make him rich? Certainly the trip leader was right when he complained that Ken's truancy, occasional missed signals, and faulty ace adjustment were costing the team money. But the beauty of Al's system was that it could thrive in spite of these mistakes. Studying the operation carefully, Ken saw that Francesco's gambling organization was a model small business. Profit potential in this low overhead operation apppeared limited only by the size of the team's capital investment and ability to stay in the casinos' good graces. In effect, every employee of the gambling enterprise was a stockholder; profits and losses were calculated in direct proportion to each player's capital investment. But a losing session never forced anyone out, for the B.P.'s remained so confident in the system that they vied to extend credit to any counter who didn't want to put up his own cash. They were entitled to a one-third cut of the borrowing player's share of the win (or loss), which added up to substantial profit over the long run.

Counters were also paid a "basic" salary, which financed the small bets they made while keeping track of decks for the B.P. Each player was taught beforehand how to play a simplified system called "basic strategy." * Although it obviously wasn't pos-

---

* *Basic Strategy for Four-Deck Blackjack—Las Vegas:* If the dealer has a 2 or 3 up, hit until you have a total of 13. If he has a 4, 5 or 6, hit until 12. All other times, hit until 17. If you have a soft hand, hit until soft 18, unless the dealer has a 9 or 10 up—then hit until soft 19.

Double on 11 if the dealer has a 2 through 10 up. Double on 10 if the dealer has a 2 through 9 up and double on 9 if the dealer has a 3 through 6 up.

Double on ace and 7 or ace and 6 if the dealer has a 3 through 6 up; on ace and 4 or ace and 5 if the dealer has a 4 through 6 up; and on ace and 2 or ace and 3 if the dealer has a 5 or 6 up.

Always split aces and 8s. Split 9s if the dealer has a 2 through 9 up, but not a 7. Split 7s if the dealer has a 2 through 7 up, split 6s if the dealer has a 3 through 6 up, and split 2s and 3s if the dealer has a 4 through 7 up.

sible for the counters to vary their bets significantly without blowing cover (and risking expulsion), this system allowed them to play nearly even with the house in Las Vegas. Each counter was reimbursed at an hourly rate that was double their betting level. Thus, a counter betting at a $5 table made a basic salary of $10 an hour. With this compensation most counters usually broke even or came out ahead playing basic strategy. And since all team expenses except meals were taken off the top, they were effectively enjoying an expense-paid Las Vegas trip with high profit potential.

Ken realized that the tremendous bet variations open to the B.P. solved the low hourly rate problem that he'd run into while playing on his own. Even counters with a modest investment in the team bank stood a vastly better chance of coming out ahead with the group than they did solo. And, of course, the group concept also spread out the risk, eliminating the chance of any individual being forced into bankruptcy.

Central to this entire approach was Al's pretrip planning, which involved the application of mathematical formulas that had been developed which indicated the risks inherent in various-size bets relative to the player's total bank—the so-called bet-to-bank ratio. The greater the bet size, relative to the total bank, the greater the earning potential. The catch, of course, was that these bigger bets increased the risk of tapping out.

Al usually compromised on what the team called a 5 percent element of ruin, meaning the team stood a

1-in-20 chance of being wiped out against a 19-in-20 chance of doubling their bank. On most trips these percentages were only academic because the team didn't play the hours necessary to reach either extreme. Thanks to this scientific approach, the bank was generally large enough to let them ride out negative swings and usually end up ahead on a given trip. Unlike the typical underfinanced weekend player who had to head home Sunday night to report for work first thing Monday morning, the group had enough professional gamblers and unemployed counters to keep going for weeks if necessary. Furthermore, even if the bank was wiped out in one session, they would be able to raise additional cash to finance a subsequent trip. The likelihood of two successive tapouts, at a 5 percent element of ruin, was actually 1 out of 400. And thus far Al's team had never lost an entire bank.

The so-called element of ruin theory also affected the B.P.'s bet variation. The Big Players weren't called in on a shoe until the count had risen sufficiently to give the player a 1 percent advantage over the house. Mathematically, he could bet 1/150 of his bank with a 1 percent advantage and still stay within the 5 percent ruin criterion. Thus, on Ken's first Las Vegas trip, Ron's opening bets were limited to 1/150 of the $20,000 bank, or $133. As the B.P.'s advantage rose, he increased his bets with no additional risk. For example, with a count high enough to give the player a 4 percent advantage Ron could safely bet 1/38 of the bank, or $526.

While Ken worked as a counter during his first

Vegas team trip, he saw Ron utilize several additional techniques that succeeded in actually keeping the element of ruin under 5 percent. To begin with, he always rounded the betting limits downward (for example, $526 became $500 for playing purposes). In many situations the B.P. wagered substantially less than the allowable maximum calculated by the true count.* As Ron hopped about the elegant Tropicana, casting out $100 chips on hot decks, Ken compared the action to the last time he had played the club solo:

"Then I was going for broke, betting far too high in proportion to my bank, and worrying about getting wiped out. But Ron had none of that tension. Protected by a modest element of ruin, betting only in positive situations, assured of additional funds at any time, his sole concern was getting the maximum number of dollars into play. While everyone else in the casino kissed the dice and prayed for good luck he was obsessed by volume, for in the long run team results would rise in direct proportion to the total sum he could wager on hot decks.

"The B.P.'s chances of reaching his expected percentage return rose with the number of hands played because of a principle that statisticians loosely refer to as the Law of Large Numbers. Assume a Big Player is betting at an average 1.5 percent advantage over the house. If he plays for one hour (at 100 hands per

---

* The true count is the running count adjusted for the number of half decks remaining to be played. A highly positive true count means that the deck is rich in 10s, which makes it advantageous for the B.P. to hit less, while splitting and doubling down more often.

hour), his probability of winning $1 or more is 56 percent. If he plays for ten hours his chances of coming out ahead jump to 67 percent, while at 50 hours his chances are 84 percent. By playing 100 hours the likelihood of winning goes up to 92 percent, while 400 hours yield a reassuring 99.7 percent probability of winning.

"This projection was one of the reasons why Ron was in no hurry to call off the trip. Although I had to leave Sunday night to get back to work, Ron and the rest of the team elected to continue playing several more days. As I checked out of the motel, Ron returned my $2,000 share, explaining that the team was sufficiently far ahead not to require my capital. And, true to his word, he met me several days later at Henry's Fashion, a popular San Francisco financial-district bar, where he handed over five $100 bills, my cut of the $7,000 team victory, adjusted for the number of days I played."

Three weeks later Ron Reardon walked into the Stardust Hotel, worrying that security agents would expose the team operation at any moment. Fired up by his recent win in France, Al decided to don a disguise and join the other counters working Las Vegas for the team's first multiple B.P. weekend. As the players signaled Reardon, he began peeling bills off his $50,000 bankroll and putting them down on assorted hot decks. Unfortunately the long, narrow, crowded pits surrounded by spectators made it difficult for the Big Player to navigate his way between tables.

After Ron had paraded around the small bettors'

zoo for about five minutes, all hell broke loose. First Al flashed a hot signal. Before Ron could even begin approaching Al's table, Mike's hand went up to his chin. He was followed by Tony and finally Ken, both signaling the good word as each of their shoes turned hot. Ron dashed madly from table to table creating such a spectacle that the crowd began parting automatically to let him through as he accumulated racks of $25 chips. A growing contingent of fans trailed behind the winning B.P. until he finally called off the session. Ron had set a new team record—$9,600 in just 45 minutes. He was still shaking when he walked into Ken's room at the El Morocco to celebrate the victory. Everyone was elated except Al, who felt Ron should have kept going. "You guys always want to quit when you get a few dollars ahead," said the leader as the B.P. fondled his inflated bankroll.

An hour later, the counters decided to head over to the MGM Grand, the world's largest casino, to help Barry out. They spotted the other counters and immediately joined them in counting to provide coverage at every table in the huge pit. The long distances and crowds of people made Ken worry that Barry, playing beneath ceiling portraits of minimally clad goddesses chomping grapes, would not always be able to take advantage of every positive situation. But when Ken flashed the superhot signal to the B.P. at the far end of the pit, he instantly grabbed his money, shoved people aside, and scrambled over chairs to get his bet in before the deck went cold. By the end of the night Barry had won $12,000, putting the group ahead almost $22,000 for the trip.

A celebration back at the El Morocco was interrupted by Barker's declaration that he had managed to pick up $500 playing basic strategy. When a skeptical Ron asked for proof, Mike sat down on the double bed, pulled off his right loafer, reached into his sock, and came up empty-handed. "Damn, somebody took it," he yelled as he finished removing the rest of his footwear, finding that the entire $500 had disappeared somewhere between the Stardust and the El Morocco. As Barker began stomping out the door in his bare feet, Al asked where he was going.

"To look for the money," said Mike.

"Forget it," sighed the leader. "You'll never find it. Just consider yourself out $500."

A few minutes later Al suggested that the team modify the bank split in recognition of some surprising individual counting performances. At the beginning of the trip it had been agreed that his girl friend K.P. and Karen Lombardi would be entitled to only half a counter's share, due to their lack of proficiency. But Al felt their good work at all the sessions on this trip entitled them to a full share. "And," he added with characteristic candor, "I think my performance tonight at the Stardust entitles me to half a counter's share. After all, I was taking quite a risk out there for all of you."

Barry, Tony, Barker, and Ken all denounced both of Al's ideas, pointing out that it was too late to change the previously agreed on bank deal.

"I don't think you'd be proposing this," Judy yelled at Al, "if we were down $22,000."

After hearing everyone out the leader elected to back off. "I don't have to if I don't want to but I'll kill the idea."

Instead of making peace, Al's arrogance further irritated Judy, who resented the way he and the Big Players tended to treat counters as second-class citizens. Ken promptly changed the subject to the issue of which restaurant to choose for dinner. However, as they were breaking up, Ron foolishly walked over to Judy to tell her, "I happen to agree with you counters, but if I didn't, Al would not have backed down."

"That's it!" screamed Judy. "I'm going home! I've had it with you chauvinist bastards."

Judy, who had become one of the team's most proficient counters, changed her mind by morning. But no sooner had she overcome her misgivings than another problem developed: Tony failed to join her, Ken, and Mike to count for Ron at the Sahara. This was quite mysterious, since she had seen her fiancé head off toward the backup casino in a taxi after the chest signal had been passed after they had played their first session at the Mint, a garish downtown casino.

At first Judy figured that Tony had been picked up by one of those adept Las Vegas drivers who know how to turn a short hop into a crosstown excursion. They were virtually inescapable. One time a driver picked up Al at the Grand, explained the Strip was congested because all the shows were letting out, and suggested going two miles out of their way to reach the Desert Inn. It was only after he'd given the man $4 for what should have been a $1.50 ride that Al checked his watch and saw that it was 4:30 A.M. The shows had been out for hours.

But now, five hours into the session, everyone was worried about Tony, particularly Judy, who appeared to be having great difficulty keeping the count. As she sat there imagining that Tony was lying at the bottom of a bomb crater on the Nevada Test Site, Ron sensed she needed a break and called off the session. Just as Judy was walking out the door, her name was paged. She rushed back into the casino and grabbed the phone; it was Tony calling from the Sahara Tahoe. A newcomer to Las Vegas, he didn't realize the town had a Sahara of its own. Catching Ron's signal to move to a backup club, the lawyer, familiar with the northern Nevada casino, headed to the airport and caught a plane to Reno. There he rented a car and drove to the other Sahara on Lake Tahoe's south shore.

"The thing I couldn't understand," Tony told his teammates after flying back late that evening, "was why we would be playing a single-deck club."

Despite the errors made by Tony and the other counters, Al was able to call off the session two days later with a $44,000 victory. After Barry and Ron turned over their winnings plus the original $50,000 playing bank to Al, Ken drove him out to a nearby supermarket. Tired of hotel food and anxious to save money, Francesco had decided to cook dinner for himself and K.P. at her apartment. He also hoped this meal would patch things up with his girl friend, who had forced him to move out to the Westward Ho after a fight earlier in the week. Francesco, who had come down several days early to lay the ground-work for the sessions, had totally ignored K.P. When she complained, he made the mistake of telling her, "Look, blackjack comes first, tennis comes second. Everything, and I mean everything, comes after that."

As Uston parked at the store Al asked him to come help look for lasagne ingredients. Shopping with Francesco proved even more difficult than playing blackjack for him. When Ken handed over a package of ricotta cheese, Al, who was carrying $94,000 in cash, sent him back for a second brand that was 10¢ cheaper. As they walked out, skirting the puddles of ice cream dripping from the carts of customers who had stopped their shopping to play nickle slots, the leader told Ken, "The problem with you, Uston, is that you're a sucker for a pretty package."

Since the rest of the team was anxious to head home, Al put the lasagne in K.P.'s oven and went to work calculating the players' shares. Unfortunately the job took longer than the leader anticipated. He had just begun to count out the shares on K.P.'s bed when the group arrived. Finally Francesco called the members into the room one by one to receive their respective piles of $100 bills. But as soon as Barker lifted his cut up off a pillow and counted it down, he started yelling about being shortchanged. By the time Al convinced the team's senior citizen that he was not being cheated, smoke began pouring into the room. "What's that smell?" asked Barker as he sniffed the air.

"Jesus," cried Al running out into the kitchen, "it's the goddam lasagne."

"Ken," AL SAID, "you're the management expert —tell me what to do."

Although the team win was now up to $150,000, Francesco was more depressed than Uston had ever seen him during the six months that they had worked together. Looking out of Ken's picture window toward San Francisco Bay and Fisherman's Wharf, he laid out their problem.

"The problem is that as our team gets bigger and more professional [there were thirteen counters at this point], people's expectations rise too fast. I used to spend days working out an element of ruin and a bet-to-bank ratio. Now Steve Lottier, the new counter, handles all that for us on the computer at his insurance company in a few minutes. I used to have to scrape to raise a $10,000 stake. Now we go with $70,000 and counters are upset because they can't put up a bigger share of the bank. When this thing started, everyone was totally paranoid about casino security. Now you guys are down there getting drunk, chasing hookers, and spilling the whole deal to your friends. Ron even brought down some district attorney buddy to watch us. Has he gone mad?

"Every time I suggest we modify the financial arrangements to credit someone for a good job, Judy gets furious. She's stopped returning my phone calls. Christ, she may have already decided to alert the casinos about our technique. There are just so damn many things to worry about in this operation. You know, at one point during the last trip K.P. started flashing the crotch signal to the other women counters so she could borrow money from them in the ladies' room. She stood there in the middle of the casino scratching herself for several minutes and no one picked up on it. The problem is everyone is getting greedy. All of you are just sitting there worrying about your own cut and making a quick killing at the expense of the total operation. You don't appreciate how much I've put into building this operation. If we just stick together and concentrate on building the team this thing could go on for years. We could make millions."

Ken assured Al he was with him a hundred percent. But it was hard to keep his objectivity when the team won $23,000 on the next two trips and he ended up losing $360. Once again Uston's job forced him to miss the key winning sessions that would have pushed him into the black. The same thing happened to Steve, who called Ken at the exchange one afternoon to voice contempt for the team concept. Although the organization had won consistently since 1972, Steve had been far more successful playing single-deck alone in Las Vegas. "Ever since I met Al," he told Uston, "I've been losing money."

But Francesco, ever the optimist, saw a bright side to their collective misfortune. "If anyone had to lose on those two trips," he told Uston, "it should have been you two who understand the statistical swings inherent in our system."

"Thanks, Al," Ken replied, "we'll try to lose some money next time; that should make everyone happy."

Steve laughed when Uston reported this conversation with Al several days later. Thirty-three years old, partial to Brooks Brothers traditionals and rep ties, Lottier looked like a short Clark Kent. A month earlier, when the team leader had first called him to suggest a meeting, Steve insisted on a neutral location and showed up wearing a wig. He also left instructions with a friend to come looking for him if he wasn't back within three hours. The initial get-together went well, particularly because Steve had already bought Revere's book and used his system successfully in solo Las Vegas play. Al was impressed by the insurance man's background in computer science and card counting. Just before heading off on another trip to France with Barry, Karen, and K.P., Al hinted to his new recruit that good counting work just might lead to a B.P. slot one day soon.

Anxious not to overexpose the group, Al left the rest of the team strict instructions not to play in Las Vegas while he was gone. This prompted Ron to plan a trip to Panama. He tried to talk Ken and Steve into going along because of their demonstrated expertise. Although the B.P. pointed out that favorable house rules would probably enable both of them to win big, neither player felt strongly enough about Ron or Central America to leave their jobs. In the end Reardon was forced to take Mike Barker along as his counter.

As soon as all the B.P.'s left, several of the players approached Ken and Steve and suggested the possibility of taking a few trips on their own. The two men, who were clearly the most proficient counters on the team, were both intrigued by the idea. With their extensive background in computer science, these mathematical experts frequently got together to examine the team's statistical prospects over a drink at Henry's Fashion. And although they knew Al was opposed to players going to Las Vegas without his guidance, they couldn't see any good reason to let the highly trained contingent lose its edge while the leadership played in Europe and Central America. So they scheduled a Las Vegas mini-team trip. Two days before departing, Ken met with Tony, Judy, and Steve to review strategy. Their plan called for Ken to take on the B.P. role for half the trip with the rest of the group handling the counting. During the second half, he would join the counters while Steve became B.P. Although Al had resisted telling outsiders about the team, Ken argued that some non-members could provide additional cover.

To prove his point he checked into the MGM Grand on his first mini-team trip with Linda, a weekend date from San Francisco. Although she wasn't a counter, Ken knew her company would help him complete the fun-loving, big-spender role he was assuming for the weekend. After dinner they had an hour to kill before the Sands session, so Ken and Linda headed downstairs to browse in the shopping arcade. After viewing such items as a $3,950 bronze Indian chief, a $3,800 alabaster sculpture of a mare giving birth, and a $16,000 chess set resting on sterling silver castles, they headed over to the MGM nostalgia shop. Among the old props, costumes, and set pieces on sale were an $875 barber chair used in *The Man Who Shot Liberty Valance*, a $500 propeller from the Red Baron's plane, a $400 dress worn by Bette Davis when she played Queen Elizabeth, and a $300 pair of pants worn by Leo Carillo as the Cisco Kid. Although most of the items came from MGM productions, scattered about the shop were a few mementos celebrating the stars of other studios. For instance, on one table Linda found a large stack of "When

You Say Linda Lovelace for President You've said a Mouthful" bumper stickers discounted from $1 to 50¢.

When they finished exploring the MGM shopping mall, Ken and Linda took a taxi over to the Sands. As Uston walked into the orange casino, armed with $10,000 in cash, he looked over at the security office where he could make out a sign reading: WHEN YOU STAY WITH US IN LAS VEGAS, 6,228 HUGHES PEOPLE CARE IF YOU HAVE A GOOD TIME. He wondered if that sign had been there when Al and Angelo had been stripped and forced to give back $2,200 worth of winnings.

Picking up on the hot signals from his counters, the new Big Player began darting around the casino betting $50 to $200 a hand. Although everyone in the pit made jokes about this crazy high roller, Uston's strategy was mathematically sound. For weeks he had been using flashcards to memorize the sixty-one situations when deviation from basic strategy was required due to a positive deck. For example, when he was dealt a total of 14 against a dealer's 10 Ken knew he had to stand if the true count was +10 or above and hit if it was under +10. And, of course, as the true count rose he was able to step up his betting level without increasing the element of ruin.

In the sky above the pit security agents were laughing over Uston's incomprehensible style of play. But on the floor management couldn't have been more accommodating to the new high roller. By the session's end a grandfatherly pit boss named Stan Frederick came over, chatted with Ken, and invited him to lunch the following day at the Las Vegas Hilton. "There's a great deli over there," explained the official, who had come to the Sands via the Desert Inn and the gambling world of Steubenville, Ohio.

At noon the following day the two men met at the Mamchen Delicatessen. The place was done in a modified nineteenth-century saloon decor complete with leaded glass, gas lanterns, and rolltop cabinets. Atop the breakfronts were wicker baskets filled with plastic bagels and challah while long salamis hung over the mirror behind the bar and leftover Christmas garlands trailed down from the ceiling. "Some place, isn't it?" said Stan as they took a table next to a framed first-issue commemorative stamp of the 1972 Munich Olympics. "I come here for lunch almost every day."

Uston was flattered by the interest of this seventy-two-year-old Sands workaholic who hadn't taken a vacation since 1965. After finishing his shift Stan usually headed home to his one-bedroom apartment, dined on Stouffer's soufflés, Squirt, and Sara Lee cakes, watched television, and turned in early. He had no family, few friends, and had yet to visit Lake Mead, thirty miles away. He didn't even like gambling his own money.

Until recently Stan had refused to take in any of the lavishly choreographed reviews staged by the local hotels. But in January 1974 a fellow pit boss talked him into seeing the Hallelujah Hollywood extravaganza at the new MGM Grand, which had risen kitty-corner to Caesar's Palace. The Sands boss gaped as he watched the topless "glittering, glamorous, glorious girls of the great MGM Grand Hotel" trot on-stage for their opening number. Never, certainly not even in his vintage collection of National Geographics, had he seen a more impressive array of breasts.

For the next hour and a half he watched incredu-lously as the actors played the parts of Fanny Brice, Lena Horne, Will Rogers, Eddie Cantor, W. C. Fields, Jimmy Durante, Ed Wynn, Fred Astaire, Ginger Rogers, and Gene Kelly. Following four scenes from Kismet, a woman did an erotic underwater ballet with a dolphin. After that there was a parade of exotic animals, including the heavily sedated MGM lion, Tanya the elephant, camels, llamas, jaguars, and a 900-pound tiger who disappeared, thanks to the work of a handsome young magician. Stan was so turned on by the performance that he returned nearly every week to watch it. By the time he met Ken he had seen the show nineteen times.

Besides watching the Grand show and eating at the Mamchen Delicatessen, about the only other thing Stan really liked to do was mingle with the high roll-ers that came through his casino. He was fascinated by the way they bet more on one hand than he earned in a month. Not that Stan was complaining. The Sands paid him $100 per shift, or $25,000 a year, which was more than enough to meet his needs. Yet he was always intrigued by the free-spending types, anxious to know who they were, how they made their money, and why they wanted to risk it in Las Vegas.

Stan had been in Las Vegas twenty years, yet he had never seen anyone quite like Ken Uston. The gambler's schizophrenic multi-table play made absolutely no sense. After chatting politely for a few minutes about his recent prostate operation, the Sands pit boss finally popped the question. "Ken, tell me the truth. Why do you run around so much?"

"A couple of years ago," Uston lied, "I sat at one table for four straight hours and lost thirty grand. In those days that meant something to me. Of course today I don't have to worry about money. But I've never forgotten that experience and vowed never to expose myself to that kind of bad luck by staying at one table. You understand, don't you?"

"Of course, but the way you play makes me worry. You've got to play better. Do you know anything about blackjack?"

"Well, yes, a few years back I read a book by some guy named Thorp but it seemed too complicated to me."

"Yeah, it is too complicated. Besides, it's impossible to count down a four-deck game. You can do it with one deck but there's just too many cards in a four-deck shoe. One time we had three guys at the Sands who tried counting together. One kept track of aces and 10s, the second counted 5s, and the third handled the rest of the deck. But we got them out. All we did was move the joker up."

"I don't understand what you mean."

"We moved the joker up to about a deck and a half. When you do that there's no way that you can count the deck."

"What difference does the joker make?" Ken asked, feigning ignorance.

"Well, it's just impossible to use counting when the

joker's up like that. Anyway, listen, don't worry about it. What I'm really concerned about is that you're not playing good blackjack. The boss would give me hell if he knew I was telling you this, but the truth is that you shouldn't be splitting 10s. We've got to talk you out of that; it's a bad play. Also you double down against 10s and aces. That's a mistake."

Ignoring Stan's advice, Ken continued high rolling and lost steadily, even in highly positive sessions. Although he knew such negative swings were inherent in the system, players like Barker became particularly discouraged. After one losing session at the MGM, Barker, in his typical unscientific way, told Uston, "This place is no good. I'm quitting if we play here anymore." Although Steve and Ken tried to put the team in the black, they finally decided to call the session off after four days and fly home minus $1,300.

Linda, whom Ken had neglected because of his gambling responsibilities, was even more annoyed than his teammates. Although she hadn't placed a bet all weekend, she left Vegas without her cash, credit cards, identification, keys, and two valuable rings because her purse was stolen while she was sunbathing at the MGM pool. After they landed at the San Francisco airport, the AAA had to come out and make keys to unlock Linda's car. She drove Ken home in silence.

"Want to come back down with us next weekend?" Ken asked as he climbed out of the Nova with her luggage.

"Sure," she said, slipping the car into gear, "maybe I can buy back all my stuff at a discount."

That was the last Ken saw of Linda. On the subsequent mini-team trip he enforced the kind of rules that would have made Al proud—no dates, no shows, no drinking, and no blackjack playing between sessions:

"To keep expenses at a minimum we shared rooms at a Motel 6. The only player to rate private quarters was Jean Taylor, a secretary with a finance company in Daly City who had recently joined the team. Jean had dated Al until he discovered that she was forty-two years old. Francesco, who was forty-three at the time, later told me, 'I just assumed by the way she looked Jean was in her mid-thirties. Sure am glad I found out before things started getting really serious.'

"Like many of the men on the team, Al's male chauvinism had been reinforced by too many years spent at gambling tables where women were viewed as dim-witted ornaments. His blunt talk frequently interfered with efforts to establish new relationships, particularly when he tried praising women with remarks like 'Boy, you really have nice titties.' Ron wasn't much better. On occasion he would break a date with his girl friend explaining, 'I don't want to go out with you tonight. I'm going to look for something new to lay.'

"I was always astonished by the good-natured way in which most of the women counters managed to tolerate the piggish ways of our macho leader. Yet in a sense Al was certainly more liberal-minded than most casino bosses, who actually believe that women are incapable of playing good blackjack. In fact, Al had exploited this prejudice to the team's advantage, for he knew that women counters were less likely to be watched by pit bosses, who felt they couldn't tell the difference between a hard and soft 17. Thus, making them an integral part of the team helped provide important cover.

"This was all part of the leader's master strategy. In trying to ferret out suspected cheaters, the casinos always looked for patterns. One reason Al stacked the team with such a wide variety of players was to make it harder for security personnel to link us. Who could imagine a gang composed of men and women ranging from twenty-three to sixty-two that included engineers, used car salesmen, teachers, tellers, stock brokers, insurance men, waitresses, business executives, accountants, stewardesses, computer experts, and unemployables?

"The only major personnel problem was that women counters felt they were being exploited by the B.P.'s, who were taking the largest share of the bank. Their call for all team members to enjoy an equal share made sense to me. Determined to establish a new participatory democracy, I insisted that everyone on our mini-team split the bank up evenly. 'There's absolutely no reason for the disparity between counter and B.P. shares,' I argued convincingly at a meeting prior to our first session."

The mini-team began with a $12,500 bank, allowing the B.P. to bet $100 to $350 per hand while maintaining a 5 percent element of ruin. From the start of this trip Ken exercised tighter discipline over the counters than Al ever did. He scheduled long sessions, made sure no one played during after-hours, and imposed curfews that prevented anyone from seeing shows or raising hell. Had Al tried this sort of thing when Ken was counting, he would have rebelled instantly. But now he was a small-time Big Player with responsibilities and a payroll to meet.

Unfortunately, these strict policies didn't help Uston much at the tables. Although he won steadily at basic strategy while counting for Steve, Ken simply couldn't pull ahead as a B.P. Fortunately Steve's wins more than offset Ken's losses, giving the team a total win of $4,500.

The day after they returned to San Francisco, Ron called to report that he'd just come back from Panama with a $5,000 win. Inspired by this success, Barker had elected to stay on playing solo. Ken gave Ron hell for leaving their inexperienced teammate down there by himself. After all, Mike had still not completed the transition from compulsive gambler to smooth system player. Undercapitalized, the counter usually appeared more concerned with his own win or loss at basic strategy than with team results. Barker's attitude infuriated Al, who believed he was losing track of the count and missing signals due to his preoccupation with his own performance. After one session when Mike boasted about his small basic win in the face of a substantial team loss, Al told him, "From now on, counters are not to mention their win or loss at basic to me or any of the B.P.'s."

Ken reminded Ron of this, adding, "The guy is too compulsive to be trusted on his own. Two months ago we caught him buying keno tickets in Las Vegas." As it turned out, Uston's worst fears were justified.

In Panama Barker had bet too high in proportion to his total bank and came home a few days later minus the entire $3,000 stake he had withdrawn from his family savings account. His troubles began when the count skyrocketed and he spread to seven hands of $50. The dealer promptly hit blackjack and took the entire $350. Instead of reducing his bet size, Mike continued spreading the table on the superhot count and was out of business within an hour.

Ellen Barker was not pacified by Mike's claim that the $3,000 setback was only temporary. "What are you going to do on the next trip," she asked her husband. "Put our house up for collateral with the casinos?"

"Everything's OK," he replied. "Al's loaning me my share."

"And what happens if you lose?"

"We won't."

"That's what you've been telling me for thirty-five years."

"But this is different, honey. I've explained it to you. This isn't gambling anymore. This is a team. We're disciplined, we've got a sure thing, we're winning. There's no way we can lose. Al's got it all figured out."

"Oh, you'll all screw it up somehow. You'll all get greedy and that will be the end of it."

"No, this time we're going to put it to those casinos that are always cheating the little guy."

"Maybe, but all I know is after all the years you've been going to Las Vegas, they're still building bigger hotels and we're still sitting in our little house beside the freeway, clipping 7¢ off bathroom tissue coupons."

While Barker was being wiped out in Panama, things were going well for Al and Barry in Dieppe. The owner of the casino there was so delighted to see the men and their girl friends back in France that he invited them over to his home for dinner the night they arrived. The owner's wife served bouillabaisse and even went to the trouble of playing her old Wayne Newton records after dinner to make her American guests feel at home.

But after a couple of days at the tables the team began wearing out their warm welcome. Vastly improved counting by Karen and K.P. was a great help to the two men as they alternated B.P. responsibilities. Betting the club limit, they had pushed their win up to $158,000 when the ashen club owner finally called Al into a back room to confess he couldn't pay off. The rest of the team was forced to watch television in their hotel for several days while the two men negotiated. The leader demanded a full cash settlement while the Frenchman pleaded for understanding. "Look, there is no way I can raise all the money now. If you force me into bankruptcy it will be ten years before you get anything. Let me write you a check for $158,000 now. I have a close friend who would probably buy it from you for 80¢ on the dollar."

Al rejected that idea. Finally the players left with a check for $20,000 and a casino receipt for the balance. Their plan was to give the owner a couple of weeks to raise the money. But when Al discovered he couldn't cash the $20,000 check at a single bank in Paris, he headed back to the small club. After three intensive days of negotiations, the owner gave the leader $100,000 in francs (which he had raised through a distress sale of his $200,000 country house) and three postdated checks totaling about $40,000. The other $18,000 was written off.

Al returned to Paris with the foot-high stack of franc notes in his camera bag. After a triumphant team luncheon he headed for a bank, only to find that currency regulations prohibited changing this large sum back to dollars. Everyone was frantic except Barry. "Let's keep on playing and worry about the money later," he advised. The group headed south, finally ending up at a casino in Divonne, near Geneva. After finishing the session, Karen suggested that Al try converting 5,000 francs back to dollars at a small local bank. The teller refused but whispered that they might be able to solve their problem across the Swiss border. Only then did the team drive into Geneva, where they quickly converted the money into dollars.

"Al," Ken asked after the leader finished telling him about the trip on his return to Albany, "how could you be a professional gambler for all these years and be unfamiliar with Swiss banks?"

"I don't know," the founder said, "I've been asking myself the same question."

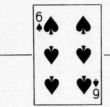

465.070   *Swindling and banco-steering: Penalties.*

1. Every person who, by color, or aid of any trick or sleight-of-hand performance, or by any fraud or fraudulent scheme, cards, dice or device, shall win for himself or for another any money or property, or representative of either, shall be punished by imprisonment in the state prison for not less than 1 year nor more than 10 years, or by a fine of not more than $5,000, or by both fine and imprisonment.

—*Gaming Crimes and Liabilities*
Nevada Revised Statutes

"I HATE TO THINK HE'S DISHONEST," Steve said, "but dammit, something's wrong with Ron."

All summer and fall Mike had been trying to convince the rest of the team that Ron might be skimming. They ignored the idea as nearly all the other suggestions he made. But this call from Steve couldn't be easily discounted.

"What do you mean?" Ken asked.

"Are you happy with his results?"

"Well, he's lost, if that's what you mean. What do you think? Is he a poor player—or is it something else?"

"I really don't know for sure."

"Do you think Ron's been cheating us?"

"Possibly. Look at the results of the six Las Vegas trips where Ron has been one of our two B.P.'s. Overall the team won $137,000, but all the money was made by Barry. Ron actually lost a total of $19,000 in the sessions he led."

By themselves those figures were inconclusive. They had to be put to what statisticians call a t-test.

"Steve," Uston said, "give me about a half hour. I'll get the data on Ron's total number of hands, average bet size, and figure his standard deviation from his 'expected value.' "

Putting aside the depository dividend analysis he'd been working on, Ken turned to this decidedly more interesting project. After fifteen minutes, he calculated that Ron's results were outside the "two sigma" range; they were actually about 2.46 sigma. In layman's terms that meant the chances of his losing as he did were about 1 in 100.

When Uston called Steve back with the bad news, Steve replied that there could only be four explanations. "Either he's a poor player, the casinos have been cheating him and not Barry, he's been skimming, or there's something else going on we don't know about." Reviewing these possibilities they both concluded that skimming was the probable explanation.

Steve quickly passed the information on to Barry,

who decided to devote a day to reviewing the matter with Al at his home. Although no clear losing pattern emerged, they came to some disturbing conclusions about Ron's financial condition. Al, who knew a good deal about Ron's past and present net worth, was troubled by his high life-style. He had no regular job, little if any savings, and was putting all his team winnings back into the playing bank. Yet he could afford heavy alimony, an expensive car, a lavish apartment, and loans to other counters. Moreover, one player had overheard Ron offering to stake his girl friend to a blackjack trip to Panama, not an inexpensive venture.

Originally Al and Barry were planning to join Ron on the Central American gambling expedition. But after completing their review and concluding that the suspect B.P. had been living on "their" money for the past five or six months, Barry decided he was no longer interested in going. "I wonder how much of my money that son of a bitch has," Barry told Al, who finally decided the time had come to suspend Ron.

Rather than accuse him of dishonesty the leader merely said, "Because of your losses we've decided you shouldn't play for a while." The B.P. took the news of his early retirement gracefully, pointing out that he had been thinking of leaving the team himself. To smooth things over and keep Ron from turning the team in, Al promised he could continue putting up bank money for several counters he had trained. That way he would still enjoy a stake in the team winnings.

Although no one ever had proof that Ron had been

skimming, most of the team were glad to see him go. "I'll bet he took us for $60,000 or more," Barry told Uston several days later. But Ken tried not to be too negative toward Ron, since it was obvious to everyone that the B.P.'s ouster would open the door for Ken—a possibility he'd been awaiting for months. The opportunity finally came one morning in late November when Al reached him at the exchange.

"Ken, we're going to make another trip, probably on the twelfth, and you might be one of the Big Players, depending on whether or not we can get enough counters."

The timing was perfect. Thanks to a team win of $37,600 on two November trips to Las Vegas, Uston's total playing bank had nearly doubled to $6,000. That personal upswing was partially due to a concession Al had made in view of the losses Ken had sustained because he'd been unable to stay for all the team sessions. Francesco agreed to pay him a share of the total team results based on the amount of time played. If Ken joined 80 percent of the sessions he would get 80 percent of a counter's share of the total win or loss for the entire trip. Thus Uston's cut would be based on a larger volume, thereby increasing his profit potential. This new arrangement plus an impending opportunity to put up a bigger share of the team bank as a Big Player led him to sit down and calculate his financial potential:

"The results were encouraging. If we started the next two trips with a $90,000 stake, there was a 19-in-20 chance that we would win from $30,000 to $150,000. And the odds were 2 out of 3 that the total would fall in the $60,000 to $120,000 range. Assuming we came out around $90,000 ahead, my personal bank size would soar to $20,000. And even if we lost $25,000 on both trips, I would still have $5,000 left. Once again the beauty of the team operation was brought home to me: high profit potential with minimal risk. It sure beat playing the stock market, where I had lost consistently over the years.

"Flying down to Los Angeles for a business meeting the day before Thanksgiving, I began wondering why this enormous potential couldn't be translated into a full-time operation. Several members of our team were professional gamblers, a number of counters were unemployed, and others would probably be willing to quit their jobs. By renting a Las Vegas apartment it would be easy to keep half a dozen of our fifteen trained counters in town on any given day. The B.P.'s could then fly in on a rotating basis and keep the team going six or even seven days a week.

"Over drinks at the home of a Los Angeles friend interested in becoming a counter, I began mapping out the potential. Beginning with a $100,000 bank and a $500 to $2,000 betting level, the full-time operation could make $100,000 a month after expenses. When the bank reached $240,000 the B.P.'s could bet $1,000 with a 5 percent element of ruin on a true count of 3 instead of 4.* Likewise they could bet

---

* Up to this point B.P.'s did not begin playing a deck until the true count (the running count adjusted for the number of half decks remaining to be played) reached +4. This policy kept the element of ruin down to 5 percent. With a larger bank, however, it would be possible to maintain this element of ruin with a lower true count, since the individual bets would be a smaller portion of the team's total playing capital.

$2,000 on a true of 5 instead of 11. Thus we would be able to make larger bets more frequently, which would benefit team cover while netting us about $200,000 a month. If the operation could survive at this level for half a year, Al, Barry, Steve (who was also being promoted to B.P. on this trip), and I would make $250,000 apiece. If our system survived a year, all of us would be ready for early retirement.

"The following day I called Al to outline my get-rich-quick scheme. He listened politely, but it was obvious he wasn't really interested: 'Ken, I think things would run a lot smoother if you concentrated on proving yourself as a Big Player and let me be chief executive officer.'

"Taking his advice, I spent the week prior to the trip studying the flash cards, counting down decks, working on ace adjustment, calculating true counts, and playing four-deck. I also went out and bought a $200 leather jacket, iridescent slacks, some silk shirts, and three-inch high heels that would elevate me to six feet, making it easier for me to spot our counters.

"To complete the B.P. outfit, aimed at making me look like the typical Las Vegas high roller, I purchased a flashy fake diamond ring in a variety store and a gaudy gold watch, which I located while driving down Columbus Street, a few blocks from my apartment. The salesman was an elderly gentleman who flashed an Omega Electra watch out the window of his battered Cadillac. Intrigued, I pulled over to the curb and began intensive negotiations for the timepiece, which was adorned with numerous "diamonds." The sticker price said $950, the man wanted $100, and I finally talked him down to $50. Just before leaving for Las Vegas several days later, I called an Omega dealer to find out how much of a bargain I'd gotten on this obviously hot timepiece. He told me the Electra model was a counterfeit worth about $10.

"When Al picked me up at the Las Vegas airport Thursday evening, he immediately asked about the flashy watch. 'Don't take it so hard,' he said after I told him the truth. 'You may have lost $40 but you've bought yourself some beautiful cover with the bosses.'

"As the leader drove me over to the Royal Las Vegas he explained that I would definitely be a B.P. for the entire trip. Barry, who was cruising with friends off the Baja California coast, had just wired word that he wouldn't be able to make it back in time for the impending trip. That left me and Steve in charge. Al decided that I would start with a session at the downtown Union Plaza, with the nearby Mint serving as our backup club. Rules and conditions at the Union Plaza were somewhat less favorable than at the major Strip clubs. Dealers at the big downtown clubs hit on soft 17, approximately a .2 percent disadvantage to the player. Crowded tables made it harder to get bets in on hot decks, and because the downtown establishments were not generally frequented by high rollers, the pit bosses tended to watch our Big Players very carefully.

"When we reached the motel Al handed over $9,000 to supplement the $6,000 bank share I had brought along. After checking into the room I changed from my three-piece suit into the new B.P. outfit, tucking $5,000 into each of three leather jacket pockets.

Downstairs I hailed a cab to the Union Plaza. As we headed down the Strip past club signs wooing gamblers with promises of 66¢ breakfasts, 88¢ lunches, $1.19 dinners, and free antacid, I nervously kept looking down at my jacket pockets to be sure none of the $100 bills were peeking out. Trying to strike up a conversation, the driver mentioned that police were looking for a man wearing a light brown leather jacket just like mine. 'Say, you're not him by any chance, are you?' he asked, turning around to get a better look. Just in case the driver was tempted to call the police and give them my whereabouts, I told him to let me off at the Lady Luck instead. I hid behind a wall of slot machines till the taxi pulled away."

Then Ken walked down Fremont Street's Glitter Gulch, where determined gamblers armed with dirty coffee cups full of nickles wore sunglasses to protect their eyes from the blinding casino signs. Shunning the golden-egg drawing at the Golden Goose and the slot machine that was spewing valuable tokens onto the street in front of the Coin Castle, Ken rushed on in to the tinsel-covered Union Plaza.

Every December Las Vegas hotels vied to come up with the most lavish holiday decor. Among the best was Caesar's, which built a huge Christmas tree out of poinsettias in the elevator lobby. But despite all the ornamentation, the holiday spirit seemed strangely absent. Traditionally this was one of Las Vegas' slowest months because regular customers tended to stay home with their families. Indeed, to hype business this year some depressed casinos were offering to "help with your Christmas shopping" by handing out one pair of sheer pantyhose with every slot jackpot. One downtown club was even giving away free three-minute long distance calls to let customers tell the folks at home how badly they were losing. In honor of the Christmas spirit the Union Plaza was offering an Olds Starfire as a slot jackpot prize. As Ken watched people vainly trying to win the car, counters gradually began arriving. First K.P. took a table, followed by Mike and Al. Since none of them found hot decks initially, Ken headed up to the bar overlooking the casino to order grapefruit juice. Uston sipped his way through two refills before Al finally flashed him the hot signal from a two-deck table. Ken immediately headed down to the floor, pulled five $100 bills out of his jacket, and dropped them on the table.

"Change?" asked the dealer.

"Play it," Ken told him.

The dealer turned to his pit boss, who glanced at Uston and gave the go ahead for what turned out to be a blackjack. But after this perfect beginning to his career as a Big Player, the count immediately dropped. Unfortunately, Ken couldn't calculate the precise amount accurately because he'd been practicing four-deck instead of two-deck all week long.* Unsure of himself, he walked away.

After playing several other tables Uston caught a signal from Mike at a two-deck game with over a

---

* To calculate bet sizes, Big Players need to know the true count. The simplest method of estimating the number of cards left is to eyeball the size of the discard pile and deduct this from the original number of decks. Obviously if one deck has been discarded from a two-deck shoe, one deck remains to be played and if one deck has been discarded from a four-deck shoe three decks remain to be played.

deck remaining to be played. As soon as he put down $500 the dealer immediately shuffled up. When the B.P. blew his cover by foolishly withdrawing the bet, a suspicious pit boss, who had given Ron trouble on the previous trip, went from dealer to dealer saying, "Anytime anybody bets $500 shuffle up."

At that point Al walked by giving the chest signal to proceed to the backup club. Self-conscious about his mistake, Ken decided to put down a couple of cover bets before leaving to make the casino officials think he really wasn't counting. Deliberately searching out a fresh deck at a table near the troublesome pit boss, Ken bet $500 off the top. After winning this hand, the count turned positive, prompting him to put out another $250, double down, and win $500 more. When Ken won his third $250 wager, the pit boss became visibly annoyed. Since the high roller was willing to play off the top of the deck, shuffling wasn't going to offer the casino any additional protection. While Uston placed another $250 cover bet, the boss phoned to alert observers in the sky to watch the B.P. for cheating. Before he could complete the call Ken headed over to the cage to cash in his chips. As he walked away from the cashier the pit boss rushed over to learn his total. It was $1,500, including $250 taken through the team approach and $1,250 via diversionary off-the-top-of-the-deck tactics.

Across the street at the Mint, a club popular with tourists because of its behind-the-scenes tour of casino operations, the counters immediately began finding hot decks. As Ken put down $500 bets several pit bosses began watching him closely. At one point Barker called him in on a superhot situation with a

+48 count. Anxious to maximize this opportunity Ken put down $500 on the far lefthand spot (which the team called third base) and then reached over two other players to bet another $500 hand in the middle of the table. Immediately a new dealer came in and shuffled up. Uston withdrew his two bets, spotted Al's crotch signal, and followed him into the men's room, where the leader whispered the name of their second backup club, the Fremont.

On the way out he decided to confuse management once again by stopping at a two-deck table and asking a nearby pit boss, "Would you mind shuffling up? I understand this can be done sometimes and I'd sure appreciate it." With great pleasure the official instructed the dealer to oblige Uston. After he finished shuffling Ken put down $500. It was great cover, especially because he lost the bet. And cover was now what Ken was most concerned about:

"As I walked into the Fremont ahead about $2,000 for the night I worried that something about my play was prompting the bosses to order shuffling-up. Blowing two clubs in 20 minutes was not the way I'd planned to begin my B.P. career. And when I started putting down my $500 bets on hot decks at this relatively uncrowded casino the pit bosses again started to watch me intently. Their possible suspicions added to my problems in handling the two-deck tables. When Al brought me in on a two-deck game the true count following my first bet remained over the required +4. Totally confused once again by the discard pile I walked away instead of putting down another $500.

"Fortunately several of the other counters began calling me in on four-deck games where I began winning steadily. Equally important, the pit bosses did not order a shuffle-up. Convinced they had a new high-rolling sucker, the pit bosses began offering me free drinks and virtually anything else I wanted.

"As I continued winning, the bosses brought over chip racks to carry the piles of $25 chips accumulating in front of me. After about two hours, I had three $2,500 racks and decided to call off the session. I strutted to the cage, knowing my first B.P. session had been highly profitable. While I was cashing in my $8,000 win, a pit boss came over, introduced himself as Harold, and encouraged me to deposit the money 'for my own protection.' This suggestion, a common method of persuading winners to return and give the casino a chance to recoup, was ideal from the team standpoint. Now I was welcome back for more profitable play without the threat of being shuffled on."

Anxious to celebrate after the session, Uston phoned up his friend Jean, who agreed to meet him for a drink at her favorite hotel, the Circus Circus. As far as she was concerned, nothing else in town could top the club's schmaltzy Baldwin organist who accompanied the trapeze artists, bicycle-riding monkeys, lion tamers, and other performers who worked in the midst of the giant tent-shaped complex. As they walked past the carnival games, Skee-Ball booths, shooting galleries, and popcorn stands lining the perimeter of the giant stage, Jean hummed to the music. It did almost as much for her as John Denver.

But after they left the casino and walked over to

Ken's motel room Jean grew somber. "What's the problem?" he asked while they walked into the room and hung up their coats.

"Ken," she said, "I'm worried about you."

"What do you mean?"

"People are talking."

"Who?"

"The pit bosses, the dealers, the shift managers."

"How do you know?"

"Well, after we met, one of the pit bosses stopped me in the Union Plaza and started pumping me for information about you."

"What did he want to know?"

"Everything. Who you were, what you did, what you said."

"Did you say anything?"

"No, of course not. Ken, I don't know what your game is. But you better watch it. They're following everything you do."

"All I'm doing is playing blackjack like anyone else."

"No, that's just it. You don't play like anyone else and the bosses are nervous. They don't like players they can't understand. Listen, I live here. I know these guys. They don't like surprises."

When Uston met with his teammates the following morning he made no mention of Jean's warning. The group decided to head back to the friendly Fremont, but different counters—Judy, Tony, and Karen—were to go along to help protect team cover.

"In the cab on the way to the Fremont I was too busy to be nervous. I quickly ran through the B.P.

flash cards twice to make sure the numbers were firmly in mind. Then I carefully arranged the stacks of $100 bills in my pockets. The previous night I'd lost track of how much cash I'd gone through. I therefore worked out a system where I would place $5,000 packets in various pockets and work through them in sequence, reserving my right jacket pocket for chips.

"Again the Fremont offered ideal conditions. As soon as I arrived Harold ran over and gave me the typical pit boss glad hand, still convinced that I'd lose in the long run. After waiting a few minutes I caught Judy's hot signal and moved in. While she flirted with the dealer, who seemed more interested in peeking down her dress than in the deal, I began winning steadily. Alternating between her table and Karen's, I went up about $5,000 within 20 minutes.

"At that point Tony brought me in. Even though I was betting $500 a hand, the casino, unaccustomed to high rollers, was still refusing to let me have $100 chips. As a result, I was forced to lay out three-and-a-half-inch stacks of $25 chips on every play. When I won these bets I was paid off with new stacks of greens. Then the true count escalated; I spread to four $500 bets and won them all. By now the running count had soared to an incredible +50 with one and a half decks remaining. The true count was 18, which meant my advantage over the house had jumped to 5 percent. I laid out five bets and Tony cleverly hesitated before putting out another bet.

" 'Sir,' I asked, 'are you going to be playing this hand?'

" 'No way,' he replied, 'not me. This is out of my league.'

"With my counter out of the way I put my sixth $500 bet on the same table. The seventh and last slot was occupied by an elderly Oriental gentleman who glanced at all my money, thought for a second, and finally pushed out a $5 chip.

"When play began the dealer showed a 6 up-card. On my first hand I was dealt a 20—two 10s. Because the deck was incredibly rich in 10s, I split and placed another $500 bet. The first card on the split ten was another ten, requiring yet another split and another $500. Two more cards were dealt and then another ten came out. Again a split was called for—a total of $2,000 was now down on the first hand alone. When yet another ten appeared, the pit boss stopped the action, telling me, 'We only allow four splits on a single hand.'

"I played the rest of the hands, one of which was a blackjack. The dealer turned over his hole card, a 10 for a total of 16, took the required hit, and busted with a face card. His hand shaking, he immediately began breaking out the black chips to pay off my $4,750 win.

"By this time Harold and several other pit bosses had surrounded the table. Now they weren't smiling or joking with their sucker. Despite all the 10s played, the running count remained sky-high at +62 with about three-quarters of a deck remaining to be played. The true count was +40, giving me an extraordinary 12 percent advantage. Again I put out six $500 bets. The Oriental man in the seventh slot watched the scene motionlessly. When he failed to make a move I placed a bet on his spot. Now I had $500 covering each of the seven spots on the table and play began.

"The dealer drew a 7 up-card; again my first hand was two 10s. Although the deck was far beyond the true count required to split, I hesitated for about 15 seconds before deciding against calling more attention to myself by making this very unorthodox play.* But I did proceed to make conventional splits and resplits, as well as double downs, on several of the other hands. After playing all my hands there was $6,000 on the table. By this point other action in the pit had ceased. Even our counters stopped playing as more than sixty people elbowed each other for a better view of my table.

"Forcing myself not to betray any nervousness after playing my hands, I leaned back in my chair, took a deep breath, let it out very slowly and told the dealer, 'I've done my work, now it's your turn.' He promptly turned over a 10 for a total of 17. Unbelievably, all twelve of my hands won, paying a total of $6,000. As the black and green chips began stacking up on my table, I asked Harold to send a club photographer over for a victory picture. He refused. Despite his bad vibes, I felt remarkably relaxed.

" 'Well,' I announced to the assembled crowd as the dealer finished counting out my winnings, 'this sure beats the hell out of going to the movies on a Saturday afternoon.'

"I played a few more hands and then gave Tony the chest signal calling off the session. When I had trouble picking up his racks of black and green chips,

* Splitting tens, a play laughed at by most neophytes, is actually warranted with a sufficiently positive count. B.P.'s would split 10s if the dealer's up-card was 2 through 6. Theoretically 10s should even be split against a dealer's 7 and 8 up-card. However, B.P.'s never made this unusual play because it endanged team cover.

Harold rushed over to carry them to the cage. I had won $27,600 in forty-five minutes, which wasn't bad for a $500-limit club. Although my take was triple my first night's winnings, no one suggested I leave my money in the cage for safekeeping. And as the security guard escorted me to the door neither Harold nor any of his other Fremont friends waved goodbye or invited me back."

When Ken walked into Mike's room at the Villa Roma fifteen minutes later, the rest of the team welcomed him as a hero. His $31,000 win for the first four sessions astonished even Al. Since Steve's group was up $8,000 prior to the start of the session that they were then playing at the Grand, the team decided to call off the trip provided Steve wasn't deeply in the red. Uston rushed over to the MGM, flashed Steve the crotch signal, and followed him into a men's room stall.

"Steve, I've just won $27,600 in forty-five minutes. Our total win for the trip is $38,000. If you're anywhere close to breaking even, let's pack it in."

"I'm up $10,000."

"We've won $48,000—let's get the hell out of here."

After hugging each other like children, the two men ran out of the bathroom, called off the session, and returned to Mike's room triumphantly to divide up their winnings. Although most of the team headed home that evening, Ken elected to stay over a couple days to unwind. When it was finally time to check out, he combined his original $6,000 bank with his $7,000 in winnings, slid it into a small briefcase, and headed for the airport.

"As the plane took off I felt slightly edgy about holding that $13,000 briefcase in my lap. And when the man in front of me stood up and started looking knowingly toward someone at the back of the plane, I began feeling paranoid. I was thinking about paging the stewardess when the man, leaning toward me and pointing toward the last row, said, 'You see that bald guy back there? He's on this flight to shoot me.'

"Without waiting for elaboration I grabbed my briefcase and walked up to an empty seat in the first-class cabin. A stewardess came over immediately and I nervously told her about the impending assassination. Instead of alerting the pilot she called another stewardess who instructed me to return to my coach seat. When I refused she insisted on sending me back.

" 'You mean I can't sit up here to avoid getting caught in the crossfire?'

" 'No, I'm sorry, but tariff regulations won't allow it.' Finally I tried to resolve the crisis by asking to upgrade my ticket to first class.

" 'Well,' she said, 'you can only do that if you have a valid credit card.'

" 'Fine,' I replied, handing over my gold American Express card. Half an hour later I called the stewardess over and asked why no one seemed to be concerned about the murder plot.

" 'Oh, you mean that guy who was sitting in front of you? No problem; he's just crazy. Every time one of us walks past him he claims we're going to stab him to death with our pens.' "

465.080 *Swindling and banco-steering: Penalties.*

2. Every person who shall entice or induce another, upon any pretense, to go to any place where any gambling game, scheme or device, or any trick, sleight-of-hand performance, fraud or fraudulent scheme, cards, dice or device is being conducted or operated; or while in such place shall entice or induce another to bet, wager or hazard any money or property, or representative of either, upon any such game, scheme, device, trick, sleight-of-hand performance, fraud or fraudulent scheme, cards, dice or device, or to execute any obligation for the payment of money, or delivery of property, or to lose, advance, or loan any money or property, or representative of either, shall be punished by imprisonment in the state prison for not less than 1 year nor more than 10 years, or by a fine of not more than $5,000, or by both fine and imprisonment.

—*Gaming Crimes and Liabilities*
Nevada Revised Statutes

"I'M VERY SORRY, MR. FRANCESCO," said the Carnelian Room maître d', "but I'm afraid this is all we have for you." Al snatched up the polka dot tie that the maître d' was offering him, draped it around the collar of his orange sport shirt, buttoned up his black leather jacket, and walked into the elegant restaurant atop San Francisco's Bank of America building.

Ever since he began taking gambling trips to France, Al had started showing a decided preference for gourmet dining. And the team partnership meeting on Monday night, December 23, was no exception. As Barry, Steve and his wife, and Ken and his hooker friend Jean (who had flown in for the weekend) were all being seated, Francesco was making sure that the waiter uncorked several bottles of expensive wine before dinner to allow them to breathe.

Although they were 600 miles from Las Vegas, Al was careful to cut off business conversation whenever waiters or busboys appeared on the scene. And of course they often lapsed into code when anyone had doubts about a dinner guest. For instance, the night of their Carnelian Room meeting Jean happened to mention that she was thinking about training to deal blackjack. To protect themselves Al, Barry, Steve, and Ken immediately began referring to counters as "dukes" and 21 as "craps." This confused Jean.

"Ken," she asked, "what are dukes and how can they help at craps?"

Frustrated over their inability to talk shop freely, the men postponed their discussion until after dinner when Al suggested that Jean adjourn to the bar with

Steve's wife so that the leaders could get down to business. As soon as they left Al asked, "How do you guys feel about having two teams, with three B.P.'s on each? Of course, we'd have to figure out a way that this would be profitable to all of you too."

The idea, of course, would naturally benefit Francesco. He'd have two teams in Las Vegas, perhaps more later on, and he'd be getting 15 percent of all the action. What was not clear, unfortunately, was how this concept would benefit Ken, Steve, or Barry. Sensing that the idea turned everyone off, Al said, "Well, it's just a thought. Put it in the back of your minds."

"Right," said Steve, "way back."

Ken proceeded to resurrect his idea for establishing a full-time operation in Las Vegas. When this failed to generate any enthusiasm, Al turned to the subject of bank size on a forthcoming trip. He suggested they should increase the stake from $125,000 to $150,000, enabling their growing contingent of counters to put up more money than they did on the previous trip.

"We're going to be taking a dozen along this time," explained the leader, "and if we don't increase the bank size, all of them will probably bitch about not being able to contribute more money to the bank."

Although Ken saw this point, he suspected Al really wanted a higher bank because it would enable him to lend more funds to counters, thereby increasing his profit potential. Indeed, contrary to Francesco's contention, some counters were actually complaining that the bank was rising so fast that they were forced to borrow from the leader to make their full share.

Uston did some quick figuring, which showed the team could earn more with a bigger bank while his own return would be about the same in either case.

"Sure," Ken told Al after finishing his calculation, "the $150,000 bank makes good sense."

Then the discussion turned to some of the other financial opportunities being pursued or studied by the four men. Barry and Al described a ramshackle 200-unit suburban apartment house they had bought and were refurbishing. They discussed the possibility of a joint blackjack bank for foreign play, with Al and Barry returning to France while Steve and Ken headed to South America or the Bahamas. Steve discussed his idea of entering the stock option field by using computer programs to detect exploitable market anomalies, as well as his notion of a computerized racehorse handicapping system, and Ken voiced his thoughts on the team opening their own casino.

Al was fascinated by the last proposal because counter Mike Barker had met a veteran gambler in Las Vegas seeking backing for a new club in the Bahamas with supposedly unlimited potential. "Fantastic. I could handle craps, Steve could take care of roulette and baccarat, Ken could run keno, and Barry could run blackjack."

"Right," said Steve, "but what do we do with card counters?"

"Drag them out by the neck," replied Barry as the waiter arrived with their $210 check.

Two days later Barry called Ken at the office to discuss the preparations for the forthcoming team trip. When Steve phoned in the midst of their talk,

Uston immediately cut him in on the conversation via the conferencing unit on his desktop key set. By dismantling the instrument and removing certain lugs, it was possible to push down all the buttons and confer with five callers simultaneously. Although this sort of unauthorized innovation was the kind of thing his former employer, the phone company, was dedicated to stamping out, it had proven useful for stock exchange work, and a godsend for the team. Any time there was a need for a joint B.P. decision, everyone simply arranged to call Ken's office at a specified time to caucus telephonically. These talks frequently spared busy team leaders the necessity of time-consuming get-togethers.

"During this particular conversation Steve succeeded in convincing Barry and me that the $150,000 bank Al had proposed would not permit bets significantly higher than a $125,000 bank. On that basis we agreed to go with the smaller sum, aiming for a $150,000 win. As I scribbled down the size of our goal on a note pad I realized this kind of objective would have been ridiculous just a few months ago. Yet now we all knew it was a real possibility.

"In view of these big stakes even the most minute details attained a sense of urgency. We agreed, for example, that the time had come to institute a number of new precautions designed to protect team cover. On the basis of my recent Fremont experience (where off-the-top-of-the-deck cover bets ingratiated me to the pit bosses and paved the way for the $27,600 win) we decided that the B.P.'s would henceforth make up to ten similar 'throw away' bets. Steve's calculations showed these cover bets cost the team only about .15 percent of our 1.5 percent, which seemed a small price to pay for such excellent protection.

"In addition, three other security measures were approved. First, counters would be instructed to give better warm signals so that the B.P.'s could make more diversionary bets before moving in on a hot deck. Second, no one would be allowed to practice on the plane, since casino officials were often heading to or from a Bay Area vacation. And finally, guidelines were to be drawn up that would restrict members from talking about the team to outsiders.

"The final measure was a touchy issue. Although part of the operation's appeal was being able to titillate friends with stories of dramatic wins, the restriction had to be enforced, since it was feared that one of the players might be tempted into giving away too much information and thereby make the team story believable. Barker had already succumbed to this temptation on one occasion. Fortunately, the friend he had mentioned it to refused to take his word for it. After listening to Mike explain how he had finally lucked into a winning system the man just scoffed, 'Mike, there is no way in the world you can beat the casinos at blackjack.' "

The new security measures plus the rest of the ideas agreed upon during the conference call were presented the following night at a team party held at Barry's home. Wisely, they waited until after everyone had enjoyed cocktails, hors d'oeuvres, dinner, and a piano player hired for the occasion—accompanied by Ken on bass—before getting down to business in the host's bedroom. Uston was amazed at how easily he, Barry, and Steve were able to sell all their proposals:

"For the first time I began to sense that the balance of power in our organization was shifting away from our founder. Although Francesco still maintained the largest financial stake (through his loans to the counters), his managerial power was now circumscribed by the other B.P.'s. No longer would the team be willing to do something simply on his say-so. The new counters were particularly independent of his authority, taking their cues from the Big Players who had recruited them.

"With $13,000 invested in the team bank I was also acutely aware of my own rapidly increasing financial exposure. We had enthusiastically named the upcoming trip *Ocean's 11* after the old Las Vegas gambling film in which Frank Sinatra, Dean Martin, and Sammy Davis, Jr. knocked out the town's power with explosives and proceed to rob several casinos; however, I was determined that our scenario end differently than the movie's. We were going to win.

"As a result I went to bed early on New Year's Eve and spent most of the following day practicing fourdeck. The rehearsal went slowly at first because it took time to get used to the higher betting level of $1,000 off the top, graduating to $2,000 and $3,000 bets as the true advanced to +7 and +10 respectively.* I began worrying that these sizable amounts might

---

* Casino limits determine the way the money was actually bet. For instance, in $500-limit clubs like the Fremont, the B.P. would simply play two hands at a time when betting at the $1,000 level. At the $2,000-limit Caesar's Palace tables, he would put down $2,000 on one spot and $1,000 on another when playing at the $3,000 level.

get us barred from some of the smaller casinos. The problem continued to bother me until finally, at 1:00 A.M., I drank a glass of cabernet sauvignon to help fall asleep. But it didn't work. I lay awake realizing it was one thing to sell the rest of the team on a brilliant new strategy. It was something else to be responsible for its success.

"I finally dozed off about 4:30 A.M., waking three hours later just after placing three $500 bets on a true count of +7 in a dream about Caesar's. I got up, packed my B.P. outfit and flip cards, put on my three-piece stock exchange suit, and headed to work. Most of the day was taken up with final preparations for the trip. Walking back to the office with $13,000 taken from my safe deposit box, I realized that within a week I would have somewhere between $5,000 and $40,000. Although Barry was comfortable with this kind of risk and could calmly watch his net worth rise and fall thousands of dollars on the turn of a single card, Steve and I both had trouble adjusting to these higher multiples."

At home in San Francisco, Barry would deny his wife $300 to repair a leaky kitchen ceiling and Ken would make only the minimum monthly payment on his BankAmericard. But in Las Vegas they led a fiscal fantasy life, tipping the maître d' $25 for a front row showroom seat, giving a cocktail waitress $5 for a cup of coffee, and throwing away more money per session in cover bets than most people earned in a month.

When they reached Las Vegas, Ken checked into the Tropicana, Steve chose the MGM, and Barry picked Caesar's. This was a reversal of Al's usual policy. The rationale was that increased betting levels on the *Ocean's 11* trip were going to raise Big Player exposure to the point where pit bosses would expect them to stay at first-rate hotels. For the three men to hole up in some cheap motel would have been inconsistent with the image they were trying to project. This new approach posed a threat to team security, but the benefits were well worth the risk. After all, there was little doubt that all three of the B.P.'s would soon win their way into the hearts and minds of the pit bosses. Not only would this give them more playing opportunities but it would also qualify Steve, Barry, and Ken for free room and board. Taking off his three-piece suit in his room at the Tropicana, Ken realized there would be no need to wear it until the exchange's budget and business plan meeting scheduled for the following Friday.

"With my B.P. outfit on, I knew I had pretty much lost whatever interest I'd ever had in the financial community. For over fifteen years in the business world nearly all my efforts were devoted toward eliminating risks and guaranteeing return. Of course I was well compensated, but for the most part everything remained so utterly predictable. The team could not compete in terms of guaranteed salaries, liberal vacation plans, disability insurance, or generous pensions. But then, none of us had joined to find security. In fact, it was the very uncertainty of the outcome that lured most of us onto the team. We knew our system was a winner; the question was how far could we take it. Every trip, every session, every hand was a challenge because at any moment we could be driven out of business.

"After changing and running through my flash cards one last time, I went down to the Tropicana where Judy, Tony, Mike, and several of our new counters were already at work. I pulled ahead about $4,000 in the first half hour before dealers began shuffling up on me. Although I tried hard to protect myself with big cover bets off the top of several single decks, I got the shuffle every time I wheeled around to bet a contiguous table with a hot four-deck. Apparently my jumping about the pit alarmed Hank, the night shift boss, who had passed the word to take countermeasures against my plays. Since it wasn't possible to play at an advantage, I flashed the ear signal to proceed to our backup club, the Sahara, and cashed out about $900 ahead."

Heading through the Tropicana parking lot, Ken heard frantic knocking coming from inside a large camper. As he approached, several young children yelled that their parents had locked them in four hours earlier promising they were only going to gamble at the club for half an hour. One of the kids was particularly upset because she desperately needed to go to the bathroom. Uston went back into the club and told an assistant manager to page the parents; he then took a cab to the Sahara. Finding the club hopelessly crowded, he returned to the Tropicana where he made a big show of tipping whenever possible. As one waitress brought him a cup of coffee he handed the dealer a $10 bill telling him, "Give me a couple of nickles," and then flipped one of the $5 chips her way.

"Hey, honey," yelled the pit boss, "maybe he would have given you the whole $10 if you had moved a little faster."

This sort of ostentation worked perfectly in the sedate, blue-domed, chandeliered casino. Soon a pit boss, who introduced himself as Jeff Allen, was making small talk with Uston.

"Where you from, Ken?"

"Well," lied the Big Player, "I have a house in New York, a house in Connecticut, and an apartment in San Francisco—so you tell me."

Half an hour later casino manager Ralph Owens showed up, handed over his card, patted him on the back, and said, "Ken, whatever you need, just ask. We want you to stay here and we'll take care of you."

While thanking Owens for this, his first big-time comp, Ken began to feel that perhaps there was no real reason to get into the Bahama casino deal that Barker's friend was talking about. In effect, the team operation was the equivalent of a small casino, with the players enjoying a dependable 1½ to 2 percent advantage on all their play. And the marvelous thing was that the group functioned virtually free of overhead. They didn't have to bear the cost of pit bosses, dealers, waitresses, security, junkets, shows, utilities, public relations, advertising, or real estate taxes. Their only real costs were plane fares and motel expenses. Ironically, the team's biggest expense, the care and feeding of the B.P.'s, was now being picked up by the friendly casino opposition (Steve and Barry had also been comped by this time at the MGM and Caesar's Palace).

After ending the first three-hour session ahead another $3,000, Ken caught a cab to the Westward Ho Motel, where he found the all-clear sign—a yellow

Wilson tennis ball can—sitting in Al's window. This simple device was the leader's way of letting everyone know it was safe to enter. Thus far they had never encountered any security problems in the small motels, but if there were a problem, the can would disappear.

At the meeting the team found that they were up a total of $10,000. But working out future playing schedules, reviewing counters' signaling errors, and deciding who could share cabs with whom proved confusing. The expanded organization (three B.P.'s and sixteen counters) was certainly impressive to see, yet it was also proving more difficult to manage. In the midst of the discussion, Mike and Tony started screaming at each other in the corner.

"You turkey," yelled Tony, "if you don't stop jumping up and down and smiling every time the B.P. wins you're going to blow it for all of us."

"No little shit like you is going to talk to me like that," screamed Mike.

"Fuck you."

After the other players broke up the sparring match, Al tried to pacify everyone with small Dixie cups full of wine poured from two bottles that had been breathing on his dresser for several hours. But when Mike asked for a refill the B.P. turned him down: "You guys have to play tonight."

Always parsimonious, Francesco seemed to be turning downright miserly on this particular trip. He kept track of every last dinner check, hounding every player to repay whatever he'd advanced for them. Although Barry, Steve, and Ken all picked up the restaurant tabs for Al after post-victory dinner celebrations, he refused to reciprocate. And despite the fact that he often carried over $20,000 in cash, the leader continually borrowed dimes for pay phone calls.

The founder's conservative fiscal policy surfaced the following morning when Barker asked him to contribute $10 toward a team wedding present for Tony and Judy. The counters were getting married at four that afternoon in the Chapel of the West next to the Frontier, and Barker wanted to get a special gift for them—a $225 plastic toilet seat inlaid with valuable uncirculated coins from the 2001 Space Odyssey Shop in the MGM basement. But Francesco thought that was ridiculous: "It would be a hell of a lot cheaper to buy a $5 seat at Sears and lay the coins down yourself."

Despite the fact that Al was only willing to chip in $5, Barker raised the $225 by 3:00 P.M. Unfortunately he got sidetracked at the craps tables on the way out of the Grand. This caused problems for Tony, since Mike was his best man. At 4:20 P.M., just as the minister pointed out that two more couples were waiting their turn, Barker raced into the chapel. "Sorry," he whispered to Tony, while handing over the ring, "but I hit a streak at the MGM and won $1,820."

After the ceremony everyone headed over to Caesar's Palace for a wedding dinner at the Bacchanal. As soon as the team was seated, the restaurant's vestal virgins came up behind each chair and delivered a warm-up massage in preparation for the $24 prix fixe dinner. After the seven courses, accompanied by three wines, were completed, the toga-clad virgins returned to deliver a second massage.

Although most of the team felt drowsy after the heavy meal, Judy decided to celebrate by heading over to the Flamingo, Las Vegas' first major casino. Opened the day after Christmas 1946, less than six months before its founder Benjamin "Bugsy" Siegel was cut down by nine bullets at his mistress's home in Beverly Hills, this hotel was Judy's favorite Las Vegas casino. She had won there on her own in the past and did well again this evening as she moved through the pit in her wedding gown. After she had finished the session $3,200 ahead an admiring pit boss congratulated Tony: "You've got yourself a good bride."

The next morning Al and the other B.P.'s convened in Ken's hotel room for a special meeting. Their guest of honor was Barker's gambling friend Ed Saunders, a Las Vegas resident in search of backing for a new Bahamas casino. This emaciated entrepreneur, who supported himself at the local blackjack tables, arrived with his wife Joanne. Ed, who appeared to be in his mid-fifties, propped himself up on Ken's bed, explaining that he was recuperating from recent abdominal surgery: "The truth is I shouldn't even be out of the house but I like you guys and I want to help you."

Al, who had grave misgivings about meeting inside hostile casino territory (instead of at his comparatively secure motel room) was immediately suspicious of Saunders, who had a knack for turning sentences into rambling monologues and ducking tough questions with irrelevant digressions. The players learned how the Mafia had muscled in on a private game Ed had dealt to Miami millionaires, how he had plucked blackjack turkeys clean in Atlantic City, and how he had helped the Allies win World War II. After gambling and military history, Ed's greatest interest seemed to be revolutions: "I've studied all the great ones. I bet most of you don't know the real reason why the Russians put Kerensky into power after throwing out the Czar."

"Because he knew when to split pairs," said Al.

Sensing their collective impatience, Ed realized it was time to take up the casino issue. He explained that the operation would be built on a popular resort island. But when asked for details, Saunders seemed unable to provide any clear answers.

"How much money would we need?" asked Steve.

"Almost nothing," replied Ed.

"Well, it would cost something for tables, furnishings, leases, and so forth. How much would you think?"

"You fellows would know more about that than me."

"Wouldn't we have to have knowledge of casino management, craps, keno, and roulette?" asked Al.

"Not necessarily. You can do anything you want."

"What games would we have?" I asked.

"Anything you want. Find some high rollers and fly them in. We'll take care of the local officials to keep them friendly."

"In other words," Al said, "you're looking to set up an operation to cheat high rollers."

"Well, I wouldn't go that far."

Having devoted all their energies to beating casinos legitimately, none of the team leaders could generate any enthusiasm for becoming ripoff artists.

"After all," explained Al, "I don't like to cheat people."

As soon as he realized he wasn't going to get any support for his dream club, Ed began trying to sell the men a system that he claimed was twice as effective as Revere's: "I'm not particularly interested in giving this thing away, but I like you guys and I want to see you make it big."

"How much do you want?" Al asked.

"Five thousand, cash. But please understand it's not the money I'm after. I'm only charging because I figure once you pay for this technique you won't be inclined to give it away free to others."

As the group tried to get some details on how the system worked, Ed would digress into an old war story or start rambling on about another revolution. Al, Barry, and Ken finally caucused in the bathroom, where they agreed Saunders might be palming off one of a number of known betting systems that gave the player a high probability of a minor win and a small chance of a large loss. Purveyors of these methods always forgot to mention that the overall return remained unaffected by betting progressions. To protect themselves they decided to ask Ed for a chance to run the system through a computer at Steve's office, paying the $5,000 price on acceptance.

But Saunders wasn't buying: "You could make up any reason not to use it. Give me the $5,000 first; then if you later come up with a valid reason not to use the system, I'll return the $5,000."

Hoping to break the impasse Ken said, "Look, I think we can trust Ed. Why don't we give him $2,500 as a compromise with the same terms."

Al shook his head. "You're speaking for yourself, not me."

Unsure of how to handle this split decision, Saunders shifted the subject once again: "Did any of you know that after eight thousand Parisians stormed the Bastille they found only seven prisoners inside?"

465.040 *Summary seizure of unlawful gambling devices: Equipment; destruction; criminal complaints.*

2. It shall be lawful for officers in executing the duties imposed upon them by this section to break open doors for the purpose of obtaining possession of any such gambling devices.

—*Gaming Crimes and Liabilities*
Nevada Revised Statutes

"WHAT HAPPENED TO AL?" Ken asked Barry when he arrived at the Tropicana. Since the club was picking up Uston's bill, he had invited the leader and his fellow B.P. to join him and Jean for a room service dinner on the house.

"They stopped him at the door."

"What do you mean?"

"As soon as he walked into the casino a guard told him to get out."

"Do you think they spotted his face from the Griffin book?"

"Could be."

Moments later Francesco called in from a pay phone outside the hotel: "Uston, you fool. I told you we shouldn't have had that meeting with Ed Saunders in your room. They're on to us."

"How do you mean?"

"Your room's probably bugged."

"No, it isn't. I've checked the place and it's clean."

"Shit, you wouldn't know a bug from a rattlesnake."

Hanging up, Ken realized that if Al was right the entire operation might be ruined; come Monday he'd be back at the Pacific Stock Exchange. Most of the Tropicana management remained friendly, but for all he knew they were merely waiting to accumulate sufficient evidence to bust the entire team. When Uston mentioned Al's fear to Barry, the young B.P. grabbed the phone to invite his girl friend Karen to come share the room service fare. "After all," he explained, "if Al's right we might as well enjoy our last free Trop supper."

Forty-five minutes later a waiter showed up with roast beef dinners, three bottles of wine, a fifth of Scotch, and a decanter of Drambuie. During dessert Steve called and Uston asked him to join the party. He knew he shouldn't have done it, but by then the liquor had gotten the better of him and, as Barry had pointed out, if the Trop was on to the team they might as well enjoy what was left of their free ride in Nevada.

Starting his second Tropicana session at noon on Saturday, Uston looked everywhere for overt signs that the group had been unmasked. When he found none, Ken asked pit boss Jeff Allen a few leading questions:

"Hey, what's the story with Hank, the night shift manager? I get bad vibes from him."

"Oh, he's an asshole. He doesn't know what's going on. He thinks you're doing something fishy, but you can't have forty agents all over the casino."

"Of course not."

"If you're casing the deck, you must either be a genius or have 360-degree vision."

"No, I just play on instinct. I understand there's a book by some guy named Thorp that tells you how to win at blackjack, but it seems awfully complicated."

"Yeah, it's complicated and it's hard to learn. It's impossible to do it against four-deck shoes."

Reassured, he continued betting for another two hours before breaking to head for the Sands. About an hour into the Sands session, Ken placed several bets on a superhot deck at a crowded table. After a young man on his left put $10 down on the seventh spot, the B.P. proceeded to split and double, ending up with $7,000 on the table. As spectators gathered around, the dealer promptly drew two cards for a total of 21, which beat all of Uston's hands. But just as he started to rake in the chips, the young player, who had been dealt a 5 and a 6, yelled, "Wait a minute, I asked for a hit."

"But you tucked your cards under your bet," replied the dealer. "That means you wanted to stand."

"No, he didn't," interjected Uston, "you put the bet on top of his cards when you moved them over to make room for my multiple hands."

"Right," said the young man. "Besides, I'd never stand on 11."

In the midst of this argument Ken's pit boss friend,

Stan Frederick, came over to arbitrate. Uston lobbied forcefully, hoping the elderly Sands official would reconstruct the hand. Giving the young man the card he wanted in sequence would not get the Big Player back all his money. But it would have saved several of the $1,000 hands.

After hearing out both sides Stan told the players, "No bet," picked up all the cards, placed them in the discard tray, and left all the bets on the table. He had just saved Ken Uston $7,000.

A few minutes later the B.P. happened to be standing behind the player who had caused the original ruckus when Stan walked up, eyed the young man suspiciously, and told the dealer: "Win that guy's stack."

On his way out of the casino Ken stopped his pit boss friend to convince him that he hadn't been in collusion with the young man.

"Stan," Uston explained, "it wasn't that guy's fault. The dealer really did move his cards and chips."

"He wouldn't have said anything if the dealer had busted, Ken. I only did it because you were there."

"Well thanks, Stan, it was the fair thing to do and I appreciate it."

Despite the Sands' outward generosity toward Ken, at least one club official was beginning to have doubts about him. He was Herb Nunaz, a forty-eight-year-old assistant casino manager who had been with the club for fourteen years. He had gotten his start as a blackjack dealer, shifting to a sit-down job in the pit box after suffering a heart attack. In his current position Nunaz bore the dual responsibility of keeping guests happy while protecting the Sands against the myriad of con artists trying to bilk the Summa Corporation. This was a delicate business, particularly with high rollers like Ken Uston.

Following the precepts of modern casino management, Nunaz saw to it that on his shift his gambling VIPs enjoyed every convenience at the club's disposal. Pit bosses like Stan Frederick were encouraged to get friendly with the Big Players. Dealers, security guards, maître d's, waiters, and bellmen were likewise instructed to cater to their every need. But at the same time Nunaz orchestrated an elaborate security network that kept careful tabs on Uston and every other high roller.

The men overhead in the sky, the plainclothesmen from the Griffin Detective Agency, and the uniformed security personnel, give the Sands one of the most effective defense systems imaginable. With the aid of their closed-circuit videotape systems, one-way mirrors, black book of undesirables, and the Las Vegas police, they have no trouble thwarting every casino's number one problem—employee theft. Because no casino can keep an exact count of every transaction, it is relatively easy for an unscrupulous dealer to join up with a player and bilk the club out of tens of thousands. But by carefully recording play at suspect tables, the skymen have found it relatively easy to crack any such scheme. And with the help of experienced floor operatives this surveillance system usually proved to be unbeatable.

Naturally, Ken Uston's wild brand of play had not gone unnoticed by the men who spent their working hours peering down through the ceiling. But no one even made an effort to begin recording his antics—there was no effective way to follow the jittery high roller with the taping system. The only way to have gotten a film record of the Big Player's modus operandi would have been to strap on a camera and follow him around the club. Fortunately that wasn't necessary for Herb Nunaz. He already knew that Uston was involved in some kind of scheme. After all, no one, not even a crazy person, bet the way he did. Nunaz was merely waiting until he understood the nature of the scheme and whether or not it was effective. Then he would make his move.

When he had finished up at the Sands, Uston headed back to the Tropicana. While his date, who had flown in from San Francisco for the weekend, dressed for dinner, he went to the casino to make half a dozen bets "off the top" to throw off Hank, the skeptical pit boss. Ken was discouraged by his reception: "I decided to test conditions by randomly throwing $500 down in the middle of a single-deck game, although I had no idea of the count. The dealer shuffled immediately. Moving on to bet a partially dealt four-deck shoe, I got the shuffle again. After it happened for the third time I started yelling, 'Why can't I get a game in here? If you don't want me to play, just let me know. There's plenty of casinos in town.'

"Failing to get any hoped for attention, I demanded to see the casino manager. When the pit bosses failed to produce him, I went over to the phone and had the man paged. There was no answer. Hurrying back to the pit, I screamed at Hank, 'Tell him I'm checking out.'

"My date was impressed as I told her of my ruse half an hour later over dinner in the elegant Le Gourmet restaurant. The casino manager never did show up to call my bluff that night, which was fine with me. I had no intention of blowing my comp and felt this show would help provide the cover necessary to stop casino countermeasures taken against me on Hank's shift. Apparently, this boss was so frightened by me that he had every table in the place shuffling on me even when I didn't have a single counter in the house."

After signing the $94 tab that would be picked up by the casino, Ken sent his girl friend off to the MGM's "Hallelujah Hollywood" extravaganza. She was miffed that he refused to accompany her. But Uston simply had to take a nap for his midnight session at the Holiday, a small casino housed in a replica of a Mississippi steamboat beached next to the Holiday Inn. The club billed itself as "Home of the World's Most Liberal Slot Machine," which naturally attracted hordes of small-time bettors. Most of the gamblers filling up the fifteen blackjack tables bet the $1 minimum, although occasionally a bold soul would venture $5.

Despite the crowded conditions, the counters gradually found room at the tables and began signaling Ken in. When he threw down $500 to play his first hot deck the other dollar bettors stared at the cash incredulously.

"Change?" the dealer asked.

"Play it."

"Five hundred dollars plays," he yelled to the pit boss, who looked Uston over and gave the go-ahead. Ken's action attracted the inevitable crowd, including one young man in a white jumpsuit who moved in to bet alongside the Big Player. After Ken split 9s against a dealer's 9, the admiring player nodded: "That's the right play."

"Thanks, I really wasn't sure."

"Who are you kidding? You know how to play this game."

"Hell, man, this game is all hunches and intuition."

Uston won both hands and continued playing. A few minutes later another fairly unusual situation came up, requiring a double down on an ace–3 against a dealer's four.

"That the right play too," said his new fan as the B.P. won again.

A few minutes later Ken was called back yet again to the same table. After watching Uston a little longer, the man in the jumpsuit said loudly, "I don't get it. A whole bunch of little cards come out and all at once you appear out of nowhere." *

Anxious to escape this observant kibitzer, the B.P. immediately headed over to the opposite side of the casino, where he chatted with the amiable pit bosses who offered him a free room in the adjacent Holiday Inn. Uston turned them down.

As he proceeded to place bets on hot decks around the pit, Holiday bosses ran from table to table break-

---

* He was referring to the fact that when small cards are dealt the rest of the shoe tends to be rich in 10s and aces, which pushes the count up to the player's advantage.

ing out the $100 chips. This was a bit worrisome, particularly when one casino official followed behind him taking notes.

"Are you keeping track of how much I'm winning or losing?" he asked his shadow.

"No. I'm just keeping track of the number of black chips left at each table. I haven't had this much fun in years."

Uston found that the other bosses and many players also seemed amused by his unconventional style:

"While playing I remained friendly with the casino officials, accepting their repeated offers of complimentary coffee or grapefruit juice on the rocks, and tipping the waitress $5 each time. Although the Holiday people kept pushing more drinks on me, I didn't think anything of it until about 2:00 A.M., when I noticed a strange taste in a fresh glass of juice. Immediately I remembered the episode in Thorp's book where he reported being mickied, as well as Al's story of a similar occurrence years ago. Frightened and unsure of myself, I wobbled off to the men's room, sat down in a stall, and wondered why I had ever left the safe world of securities.

"But within fifteen minutes the paranoia subsided, my head began to clear, and I returned to the casino, refusing all subsequent drink offers. I may have been imagining things but it seemed as though someone was pushing one sort of beverage or another at me about every ten minutes. I called off the session at 3:30 A.M. with a loss of $3,000 and walked out vowing never to sip anything again at that casino.

"Late Sunday evening I returned to the Holiday

once again after putting my date in a cab to the air-port. I had promised to drive her out but a long session at the Sands made it impossible. As the taxi pulled up I held out a $5 bill for her fare, but she refused to take it. 'Save it for one of your hookers,' she said, slamming the door in my face.

"Once again my preoccupation with gambling had screwed things up. It seemed as if all the B.P.'s were having troubles with their women. Steve had been having problems with his wife ever since he had become absorbed in the team; K.P. was still refusing to let Al move back into her apartment, despite the burned lasagne dinner; and Karen was livid over Barry's relentless search for new women.

"My graveyard session at the Holiday started slowly because bad conditions made it impossible to play more than one hand every few minutes. After being called into a crowded table near the end of a shoe and making a single bet, the dealer, almost invariably, would pull the cards out to shuffle. Despite this problem I managed to win all of my first five hands for a total of $2,500.

"After losing to the house for about ten minutes Mike flashed the superhot signal. I moved in and put down $500 on each of three open spots at his table. The young, obviously inexperienced woman dealer turned to the pit boss, got his approval, and dealt me three winning hands. With the count now up over +40, I tapped the table with a chip, signaling Mike to leave his seat. As he joined the crowd of spectators forming a large semicircle behind me I put out three more bets, then handed the dealer fifteen black chips and told her to place them on three remaining open spots out of my reach. After the only other bettor at the table pushed out his $2 wager, the dealer turned over a 5 up-card, which gave her a high probability of busting on this superpositive deck. My first hand was 20, and as I paused to study the cards I could hear someone yelling from the crowd, 'Split the son of a bitch.' I did precisely that.

"When I turned to my next hand, an ace and a 4, the same self-appointed adviser yelled, 'Double down, man.' He was right again. The next hand was a 10 and a deuce, which I tucked under my little stack of black chips. Then I pulled back a chair blocking my way, walked around to the other side of the table, and played the other three hands. The dealer had a 10 in the hole; as she slid her third card out of the shoe I could hear my number one fan yelling, 'Break, you bitch.'

"When she did, pandemonium broke out in the casino. Play stopped because the dealer didn't have enough chips to pay me off. Within seconds people from all over the Holiday boat were running over for a look. The dealer seemed baffled by the whole thing, as did the $2 bettor playing next to me; he had just busted in the face of my huge win. While waiting I thought of Ron, who used to bang the table yelling, 'Pay up! Pay up!' in similar situations. But that just wasn't my style.

"After several minutes a boss finally arrived with a rack of $10,000 in black chips to make the payoff. Since the count was still sky-high, I placed six more $500 bets. This time the dealer showed a four up-card, which was also highly favorable to the player. My first two hands were blackjacks. While studying each of the other hands, I could hear people debating about the correct play. Gamblers, pit bosses, waitresses, cleaning men, and change girls were all watching the table as I made the required double down and splits. The dealer turned over a 10 in the hole, then hit herself with a 9 to bust once again. After tipping the woman $100 I scooped up my $10,000 rack of black chips, called off the session, and headed for the cage. My win for the thirty-minute session was $9,400."

The following morning Tony phoned about half an hour before Uston's 11:00 wake-up call: "Ken, something happened up at the Holiday last night that you should know about. Do you want to discuss it over the phone?"

"No," Uston told him, "meet me for breakfast at Caesar's Noshorium in twenty minutes."

Ken liked to eat at the Noshorium, although he could never quite understand how the little coffee shop fit in with the hotel's Roman bacchanal motif. Even page 23 of the Caesar's souvenir booklet admitted that "the custom of noshing was unheard of in the Roman empire: even the renowned Cicero didn't know what nosh meant," although Caesar himself apparently felt that this ignorance was all for the best: "Think how noshing could have changed history had it become popular. I, Caesar, would not have been able to conquer Gaul and Britain if my legions had stopped every few miles along the Appian Way for a quick nosh. And would Cleopatra, the Queen of the Nile, have been as appealing to Mark

Antony had she spent her time noshing instead of being seductive?"

When Ken arrived at the restaurant the newlywed counter was fingering a glass of ice water at a table in the center of the room. Anxious not to be overheard, the B.P. asked one of the waitresses if he and Tony could move to a back booth.

"Those tables are closed," she said. "Stay out of there."

"What about that one against the wall?" Uston inquired, handing over a $5 bill.

"Of course," the woman replied as she showed the men to their new seats.

After they ordered breakfast Tony told Ken that he had picked up some bad vibrations from the Holiday people following the quick $9,400 win the previous night. In line with team policy the counters had continued playing for about fifteen minutes after the B.P. left: "As you walked out," Tony said, "the head pit boss came over to one of the officials who had been glad-handing you all night and said, 'Before he comes in here again, find out who he is, where he's from, and what he does.'

"Look Ken," said Tony, "I don't know what he meant, but they might call around the Strip about you. These guys could really hurt you. I mean what would your exchange directors say if they knew their chief financial officer was in Las Vegas gambling tens of thousands?"

"They'd say fire the guy and call in the auditors."

Although the counter's news didn't surprise Ken, the B.P. knew he had a good point:

"Already private eyes had gone to visit Steve's employer to raise questions about his gambling in Las Vegas. Although it didn't cost him his job, it did force him to give away information on the system to reassure his skeptical boss. And detectives had also shown up recently at the Georgia home of Karen Lombardi's parents, raising questions about her association with one Billy Mark (a pseudonym used by Barry in Vegas). These investigators claimed Mark was a con artist who had ripped off Nevada casinos to the tune of $100,000. Karen's parents, who were unfamiliar with Barry's fake identity, professed their ignorance and quickly showed their guests to the door. How long, I wondered, would it be before detectives began looking into my life? Perhaps they were already on the case."

After the talk with Tony Ken taxied over to the Sands to begin his noon session. His heavy betting led a number of onlookers to try ingratiating themselves with the B.P. One was a buxom, bubblegum-chewing dark-haired woman whose constant chattering disturbed Ken's counting. After he had ignored her for about ten minutes she tried to catch his eye by lunging in his direction while throwing a drink at his shoe. Acting blasé, Uston turned to the security man who had been chaperoning him and his money and said. "Hey, Eddie, get her off my back will you?"

The guard returned a couple minutes later to report. "She won't bother you anymore, Mr. Uston. I told her to take a hike."

"Who would believe this?" muttered the Big Player to no one in particular. "Now I need a bodyguard just to keep the women away from me. Goddam, I love it."

A while later he caught a hot signal from Tony. Spreading to six hands, he made several splits and doubles and won every single hand. The count went up, and he bet seven hands as the pit bosses rushed over to replenish the tray with black chips. After Ken doubled, split, and won all his hands, again the pit boss stopped the action: "Wait a minute, we've got to get some more black chips." Play stopped for five minutes as the Sands man went back to the cage to get the additional black chips necessary to pay Ken off.

"You mean the Sands Hotel doesn't have enough money to pay me off?" Ken told one boss. "Don't worry, I'll be glad to give you guys a marker."

As soon as the chips arrived Uston cashed them in, not wanting to blow any of his $8,000 win. As he walked out of the casino his pit boss friend Stan Frederick passed by. "Ken, leaving already? You just got here."

"I know," he replied, "but my stomach is bothering me and I want to lie down."

"No problem, we'll get you a room right here."

"Thanks. Maybe next time I'll stay with you."

"Anytime. And by the way, if you ever need tickets to the shows like the MGM's 'Hallelujah Hollywood,' we can set it up. Don't worry about reservations or anything. If you want I can even get you backstage at the Grand to see the dolphin."

After tucking his money away Ken caught a cab to the Riviera, where he picked up a second taxi to the Phillips 66 gas station next to the Westward Ho. This routing was all part of a diversionary approach developed by the team in view of the fact that Sands personnel had followed both Al and Barry on previous trips. Since they knew casino officials could easily get their destinations from the drivers (local law required them to note this data), the players took one cab to a phony destination and another to a location near the intended address.

Walking over to Al's motel room from the filling station, Ken found no one home. This posed a problem, because he had $30,000 in his pockets. Standing there waiting for him to return, Uston flinched every time someone passed the door. Finally the B.P. walked back to the gas station to phone his hotel for messages. Unfortunately all he had on him was $100 bills. When the attendant was unable to make change, Uston walked slowly back to Al's room. He continually glanced around to see if anyone was behind him, for he had more than casino spies to worry about. Betting thousands of dollars in front of large crowds made him a clear target for every criminal in Las Vegas. Local papers were always full of stories about muggers knocking visitors over for a mere $10. People in this town were willing to kill for $1,000 or less.

Finally Barker drove up in a Hertz Pinto with Judy, Tony, and Al. Uston learned that the team was up a total of $78,000 (Steve and Barry had each won over $35,000 while Ken was in the black for about $6,000). Although this was considerably short of their $150,000 goal, Uston suggested calling off the trip. "If we quit now I can go back to work tomorrow and save my week's vacation for a future trip."

"Quit!" screamed Al. "What are you talking about? You guys always want to quit when we're up a few bucks. Goddammit, we came down here to double the bank. We're going to stay and double it."

"But Al," replied Ken, "if we go home now we can use my vacation time for another ten-day trip next month."

"Listen, this whole thing may be a vacation for you but it's a full-time job for me and a lot of the others. This is the way we make our living. You've got a nice salary to fall back on. The casinos could put us out of business by next month. I say we keep going while we have the chance."

After the rest of the team bought his argument, Al asked Ken why he had quit a Sands session Sunday after going ahead $5,600 in 30 minutes.

"Hey, listen," replied the B.P., "I thought we were getting close to $100,000 and didn't want to risk taking a huge dumping."

"Bullshit," said the leader. "That was a half-assed thing to do."

Anxious to return to the tables, the other players began raising questions about strategy for the remainder of the trip. With the team bank now over $200,000 the B.P.'s agreed to up their betting levels, putting out $1,000 whenever possible, increasing to $2,000 at a true of +6 and $3,000 at a true of +8.

Then Ken proposed an idea called "Operation Hank," designed to convince the hostile night-shift manager at the Tropicana that Ken wasn't a counter, thereby buying additional play at his casino. The idea was simply to inundate Hank's shift just after midnight with as many counters as possible, covering every one of the ten tables remaining open. In order to play continuously, Uston would bet on warm as well as hot signals. In addition, he'd bet off the top of both four-deck and single-deck tables for cover purposes. By playing like a madman during the hour-long session, throwing out money wildly, and always having at least one bet going, he felt he could mislead Hank completely. After all, no sane system bettor would throw money around that way. Al loved this proposal, as did Ken's other teammates.

After dropping $3,500 at a Stardust session late that afternoon, Ken headed over to dine with Al, Steve, and Barry at the Hilton International's 18,000-square-foot Benihana restaurant. Samurai fighters engaged in one of their simulated duels while Francesco ordered. As periodic artificial thundershowers filled pools terraced in the Shoji tradition with fountains, streams, towering trees, and bridges, the three men did their best to overcome the language barrier with the Oriental staff. The waiter responded to Ken's order for a Kirin beer by bringing green tea. When Steve tried to get some sushi he ended up with a screwdriver. And Al's burgundy never did get a chance to breathe properly. But these and other frustrations, such as being denied a large table, were compensated for by the fact that the team was free to talk business. After all, if the waiters couldn't get orders straight, there was no way they were going to pick up on blackjack talk.

Even if they had been able to understand, none of the Benihana staff would have been impressed with the team's technique that particular night, for as dinner was served, Barry arrived looking chalk white and reported that he had just set a new team record by dropping $39,000 at the Desert Inn. He lost all his cash—$30,000—in the first two hours and was forced to return to his box at Caesar's to pick up another $10,000. Returning to the Desert Inn, he blew nearly all of that sum in just a few minutes by spreading the table with $1,000 bets. Things had gone so badly that Barry almost had to part with several rare $500 bills he'd been carrying around in Nevada, Panama, the Bahamas, and France as good luck pieces.

"Do you think you were cheated?" asked Al.

"Man, you never really know, but I doubt it. I didn't see anything, and I was really watching their hands and eyes. I kept telling them to slow down when they started pulling the cards out of the shoe fast—and they did." *

Listening to Barry narrate his horror story, Ken thought back to a day several weeks earlier when a broker friend who counted cards had come over to his apartment to discuss his favorite subject—losing. Ever since extreme negative swings had led to his personal Las Vegas wipeout several years ago, the man approached the blackjack pit conservatively. He warned Ken about the dangers of the team's escalating betting level. "Those swings are wild, Kenny. I'm telling you, they can really hurt you. Watch out. So far you guys have been lucky, but those swings are there."

* If the dealers were dealing seconds out of the shoe, they would use a fast motion to disguise their cheating.

At the time Uston brushed off the broker's admonition with some reassuring words about the team's careful element-of-ruin calculations. But now, after Barry and he had managed to drop $42,500 in just a few hours, Ken began wondering if the team's experts should have taken his cautious friend more seriously.

"Christ," Ken cried as thunderbolts shot out from the Benihana ceiling, "this afternoon we were up $78,000. Now we've lost more than half that and have to keep playing God knows how long just to get back where we were. Why wouldn't anyone listen to me when I wanted to quit?"

For the rest of the meal the men remained quiet; only the clicking of chopsticks punctuated their silence. When the waiter arrived with their check Al grabbed it, telling everyone, "I'll pay."

"You mean that?" asked Steve.

"Sure I'll pay," replied Francesco, "and we'll settle up later."

"Great," Ken told him, "Barry and I just lost $42,000 and you're worrying about your $15 dinner."

171.1235 *Gaming licensee may detain person suspected of having committed felony in gaming establishment.*

2. Any licensee or his officers, employees or
agents may take into custody and detain any
person when:

(a) Such person has committed a felony,
whether or not in the presence of
such licensee or his officers, employees, or agents; or

(b) A felony has been committed, and
such licensee, his officers, employees,
or agents have reasonable cause to
believe such person committed it.

—*Proceedings to Commitment*
Nevada Revised Statutes

As his cab flashed by the Frontier, the Sands,
Caesar's, the Flamingo, and the MGM, Ken wondered if the team would ever be satisfied. Despite
disastrous afternoon sessions the group remained
$36,000 ahead for the trip. Even a small portion of

that victory would have prompted nearly any gambler in town to celebrate.

Watching dollar bettors climb off a city bus to play the Dunes, Uston realized that in some ways losing was less of a strain in Las Vegas than winning. Despite the fact that they faced almost certain defeat, these amateurs headed gleefully into the casino. Like most tourists they would be good losers while dreaming about the remote possibility of a surprise windfall. However, the team, certain that the odds were in their favor, could accept nothing less than total victory. Even a momentary negative swing threw the players into a panic.

After the taxi dropped him off at the Tropicana, Uston headed up to his room via a side entrance, picked up a glass of wine, hurried back around to the front door, and staggered into the casino as if he had just come back from a late dinner. While wandering around the pit pretending to sip his burgundy, Ken caught a crotch signal from Tony. In the bathroom the lawyer whispered that the counters wanted to see him before starting the session. Following Tony's instructions, the B.P. headed through a rear entrance, walked through the dark parking lot, and found six glum players waiting for him in a white Fury.

"Ken," Judy began as he jumped in the back seat, "is it true that Barry lost $30,000 at the DI this afternoon?"

"No," Uston explained, "he lost $39,000."

"God! What happened?"

"He started betting to our $200,000 bank level and just got buried."

Hearing the bad news, Judy launched into the primary subject of the impromptu car conference. "Ken, you really scared us when you were playing two tables simultaneously at the Stardust this afternoon. I had to give you the count four times during one shoe. You were betting like a madman. You even played some of my negative decks."

"Look," Uston told her, "you've got to understand that when I'm in the casino, I'm on stage a hundred percent of the time. My act is to be a rich, irresponsible, fun-loving wild man, throwing money around like crazy. Every word, every movement, every bet is calculated to accomplish team objectives. When I bet two tables simultaneously it's because they're both hot and I can put more money into action. I ask you to repeat the count to avoid getting the counts from the two tables confused. When I throw out money off the top or make an impulsive bet it's merely cover designed to fake out the pit bosses."

"But Ken," said Judy, "even *they* say you shouldn't play two tables at once."

"Since when do we listen to what the pit bosses say? Only a sucker would take casino advice on how to play. If we listened to them we'd be out of business."

"Well, I don't think you should be betting in negative situations and throwing money around wildly."

"OK, I agree there. We don't have the bank we had this afternoon. I'll cool it and limit myself to hot decks."

After explaining how cover betting helped buy lucrative additional sessions while costing the team only .1 percent of its advantage, Ken said, "For God's sake have confidence in me. I know what I'm doing. I'm just trying to make our team operation last as long as possible and to earn everything I can for all of you. I'm not irresponsible; I'm just acting. Let's go get 'em."

While playing that night Ken made bets at every open table in the house. This required a departure from his customary game plan:

"With counters at every table, I moved around the pit betting the tables sequentially as the hot decks popped. We had so many counters that two of them couldn't find unmanned tables and were playing roulette together. Approaching a new shoe I'd watch the counter out of the corner of my eye, wheeling around and throwing out five black chips as soon as the signal went hot. While waiting for favorable situations I also killed time by making occasional off-the-top bets at single- and four-deck tables. After one of these cover bets, Hank, apparently convinced that I couldn't have a counter at every table, put it to me: 'Ken, what's the record length of time you stayed at one table?' I gave him the old $30,000-dumping story and continued on my way, making reckless-looking random bets.

"Throughout the hour and a half session there was no heat at all from him or any of the pit bosses. It was clear that by playing all tables I'd put my adversary at ease and established a basis for future play on his shift. I was also $3,000 ahead.

"On the way to the cashier's cage I decided to buy a little cover by throwing a $25 chip down on number

21 at the roulette table, announcing to Hank and the croupier, 'We're a partnership. If the number comes in we'll split the win three ways.'

"Faced with the prospect of sharing in an $875 win, the two blasé casino employees suddenly developed a deep interest in the little ball's progress. When the number failed to come in I turned to the croupier saying, 'Let's do it again. This time you pick a number.' Once again we lost, but both men had obviously enjoyed our game. I knew the $50 loss had been a sensible investment in public relations that would help insure future play."

The following evening Ken went over to the Riviera with Mike and Tony for a break from team play. This double-deck casino served as the team's unofficial oasis. Because there were no four-deck shoes here, the club was used solely for recreational purposes. Unlike Caesar's, the MGM, or the Sahara, the players didn't have to worry constantly about security. Customarily one member of the team checked into the hotel so that everyone else could enjoy access to the pool and get preferential tennis reservations.

Over drinks the three men discussed the nation's recent streaking craze. All over America people had been taking off their clothes and running through crowded theaters, restaurants, and auditoriums. Talk of this phenomenon soon prompted Ken's friends to dare him to dash through the Riviera undressed. Uston obliged by dropping his trousers around his ankles and mini-streaking the casino. Incredibly, his performance failed to turn any heads. Just when he had abandoned all hope of getting a rise out of the gambling-minded crowd, the Big Player was stopped by an elderly rancher.

"Hey buddy," he asked, "got a light?"

Determined to make his mark that night, Ken subsequently staggered up to the Riviera's showroom stage and danced with the Fifth Dimension. His career as the Sixth Dimension was promptly brought to an end by two security guards who politely eased him off stage. Ken and Barry then returned to the Tropicana where Ken called Jean, who showed up in his room fifteen minutes later with her younger sister Mary.

"She doesn't do anything," explained Uston's hooker friend. "She just likes to take pictures."

As Ken, Barry, and Jean undressed, Mary crawled around them with her Nikon searching for good angles. After shooting pictures for about five minutes she put down her camera and turned to Barry apologetically. "I hope my flash isn't disturbing you."

"Not at all. You using Tri-X?"

"Of course."

"What's the filter?"

"K–2."

"You don't need it indoors."

"Really?"

"Trust me."

The following morning Ken rode past Caesar's driveway replicas of *The Rape of the Sabines*, *Venus de Milo*, *Winged Victory*, and Michelangelo's *David* to begin another session. This statuary, carved from white carrara marble torn from the Italian mountain used by Michelangelo, was part of the Roman theme dominating every inch of the casino. The club's publicity office tempted tourists to the tables with promotional material urging them to "Come to Caesar's Forum Casino. Pay court to the Goddess Fortuna or Dame Fortune. Woo Lady Luck. The choice is yours. May the Fates guide your hand. Empires have been won at the Caesar's Forum Casino tables and I, Caesar, hope the gods smile upon you."

In the pit Uston found conditions excellent, frequently playing tables accompanied only by his counters. The Big Player ignored the customary crowd of spectators until he suddenly heard a familiar voice behind him saying, "Now that's the man I want to play beside." Moments later Sammy Davis, Jr. sat down next to Ken and began betting $500 a hand.

"Say, that's some ring you've got," the singer said, pointing to Uston's new Tiger Eye.

"You want it?" asked Ken.

"Thanks, but I don't have any room left," said Davis, flashing all eight of his rings at the B.P.

While Uston won steadily his new playing companion kept losing his $500 hands.

"You nervous?" asked the B.P., as Davis gripped the table rail following a double down.

"Boy, am I nervous."

"I know what you mean—white knuckles."

"Well, I wouldn't go *that* far."

When the entertainer busted, he pocketed his few remaining chips and stood up.

"Leaving already?" asked Ken, who had just won again. "Why not stay for a few more hands?"

"Thanks, but if it's all the same to you I think I'll stick to singing 'Candyman.'"

After Sammy Davis left Uston quickly found himself upstaged by a stocky Brazilian who bet so heavily that the bosses let him turn over the dealer's cards on each hand. Although the casino had a $3,000 limit, he relished putting down $6,000 stacks of chips on his spot. Both the high roller and club officials knew the extra $3,000 was strictly for show. Yet on occasion the player cleverly used this grandiose showmanship to his advantage. Ken watched from a nearby table as the man played two spots, losing a $6,000 double down and winning the second hand for $3,000. Before the dealer had a chance to react, the Brazilian pointed at the two bets, saying, "One pays the other." The dealer, confused by the $6,000 stack (which was actually a $3,000 bet) nodded and collected the cards as the man withdrew his chips.

"How come nothing like that ever happens to me?" Uston mused. But, as luck would have it, two days later, at the Sands Hotel, an even greater windfall came his way.

"When I walked into the casino, Mike had his hand on his chin, flashing a superhot signal. As I'd done dozens of times before, I walked up to the table, stopped the action, and said, 'Give me five'—casino jargon for 'Give me a marker for $5,000.'

"The dealer turned to Stan, the boss on duty, who said, 'Go ahead.' Stan then walked away from the table to the pit desk to start the paperwork that always seemed to be required when I started playing.

"The dealer began pulling stacks of black chips out of his tray. I noticed something strange: Usually a dealer gives me two stacks of 20 chips and one stack of 10 chips, totaling $5,000. But this dealer, who must have been unused to such huge denominations, arranged five stacks of 20 chips—$10,000—and pushed them toward me. I stashed them in both pockets of my jacket as fast as I could, just finishing as Stan came over with the $5,000 marker for me to sign.

"I played several hands and then moved to another table. Stan and the dealer were quietly conferring, both observing the tray. I played at three or four more tables, and then I heard Stan say, 'Ken, Ken, Ken.' There was Stan walking toward me rapidly.

"He stared directly into my eyes, giving me the man-to-man, be-honest-with-me look. 'Did the dealer give you $10,000?'

"Trying to look surprised and a little outraged, I said, 'Hell no! He gave me five. I lost three at one table, won four at another, and now have six.' There must be a God though—I lost $6,000 during that session."

Later that afternoon Ken scheduled a session at the Stardust. He continued to make his outrageous plays, bobbing from table to table. As always, his wild style attracted the eye of everyone in the pit, including one boss who watched for several minutes before walking up to Ken and whispering, "I'd like to give you a tip. I could lose my job if they knew I was telling you this, so don't repeat it to anyone, OK?"

"OK."

"If you keep playing like that, you're going to get wiped out. If I were you, I'd back off and learn the game before you put out all that money. I just hate to see you hurt yourself in here."

Ken was incredulous. "This was the only boss in Vegas I ever met who actually seemed to worry about me. Others just were out to fleece me so they could enhance their club's bottom line. This poor guy had seen me stand on 15s and 16s against 9s and 10s— usually bad plays, but in our plus decks the correct thing to do. Here he was jeopardizing his job to help me out. Hell, I was really touched."

Later that night, Ken went over to the Landmark where Steve was playing. He found Steve glumly counting black chips at a coffee shop table.

"Ken," said the accountant as he stacked what was left of his $100 tokens, "do you ever think maybe we've got the right system and the wrong team?"

"What's wrong?"

"Oh, nothing, just dropped another $12,000."

"Don't worry, it's just one of the swings."

"I know, but I'm really beginning to have my doubts about these new counters we brought along. What's the point of working so hard if they won't do their job?"

"Are you sure it's their fault?"

"Not really. It's just that every time I have a session like this I realize I could have done more for the team by staying in bed."

"Steve, hang in there. In the long run we have the advantage."

"I know that, but it's the short run that worries me. Look, having a losing session is one thing. But these dumb counters are making their signals so poorly that you can't get the count. Others are so obvious that it's only a matter of time until one of the casinos figures out our system. And when that happens it's the Big Players like you and me who stand to get barred for life. We'll be cut out of the profits just when things are really taking off."

Determined to prevent Steve's nightmare from coming true, Ken skipped his afternoon nap to lay out a B.P. pension plan. He went through several drafts before finally coming up with one that seemed satisfactory:

To: Al, Barry, and Steve
From: Ken
Subject: Barring of B.P.'s

The first B.P. that is barred will receive 6 percent of all future banks.

If Barry, Steve, or Ken is barred and a trip is taken with three B.P.'s (one of them a new B.P. replacing the barred B.P.), the formula is as follows:

First old B.P.	14%
Second old B.P.	14
Al	14
New B.P.	12
Barred B.P.	6
Total	60

If Barry, Steve, or Ken is barred and a trip is taken with two B.P.'s, the formula is as follows:

First old B.P.	18%
Second old B.P.	18
Al	18
Barred B.P.	6
Total	60

The second barred B.P. will share the 6 percent "barred bank" equally with the first barred B.P. Thus, when two B.P.'s are barred, they will each receive 3 percent of the "barred bank."

Any new B.P. will be brought in at 12 percent. If a second B.P. is then barred and it is necessary to bring in a second new B.P., the first new B.P. will receive 14 percent and the second new B.P. will be brought in at 12 percent.

In the future, all barred B.P.'s will share the 6 percent "barred bank" equally.

If a B.P. leaves the team for cause, he obviously would have no portion of the "barred bank."

Uston had no trouble selling this pension program to fellow team leaders at a meeting the following day. Shortly after the pact was ratified the group decided to call off the trip because Barry and Steve were getting heat from the Desert Inn and Landmark respectively. Ken and Steve spent the entire flight home making the complicated calculations necessary to divide up the $89,000 win. Unfortunately, when it came time to hand out the player shares in the deserted TWA Ambassador Lounge (Uston was a member), $4,000 was missing. Sitting on a couch with $85,000 in his lap Al began cross-examining the Big Players to determine what had gone wrong.

"All right," he said, after failing to get a satisfactory answer, "we'll give the counters their shares now but the B.P. cut stays in the bank until I get a confession."

During a meeting the following night at Francesco's house the four team leaders agreed the only honest way to resolve the moral crisis was a lie detector test. "I've got the perfect guy," the leader told his Big Players. "His name is Arnold Harrison. He does most of the polygraph work for the fast-food places around town. I used to hire him to track down workers taking money from my fried chicken franchise. Got rid of four thieves that way."

Uston was the first to undergo the exam. Arriving at Harrison's downtown San Francisco office, he found Al's chosen examiner in the midst of repairing his polygraph.

"Sorry," apologized the goateed man as he fiddled with the condensers, "but the damn thing broke down on me this morning while I was running through a bunch of hamburger cases."

About fifteen minutes later Harrison sat Ken down and hooked him up to the machine. Although Uston had readily agreed to the exam, he now began having second thoughts:

"Over the past few months I had charged off shows, as well as incidental items like razor blades, shaving cream, and toothbrushes as a team expense. Although taking such minor items could hardly be considered stealing, there would be no way to explain myself to the inflexible lie detector. My whole team career was jeopardized by this test."

As Harrison hooked up his subject, Uston felt more intimidated by the machine than by any pit boss he'd ever met.

"Will the test distort if I'm nervous?" asked Ken.

"No, I adjust for that in the preliminary questions."

After running down a list of simple biographical queries the polygrapher got down to work.

"Ken, have you ever stolen anything in your life?"

"Yes."

"Do you live in San Francisco?"

"Yes."

"Have you ever eaten any unauthorized Big Macs?"

"Unauthorized?"

"God, I'm sorry, Ken, I've got the wrong list of questions here. These are for my hamburger cases."

The examiner quickly straightened out his confusion, and as soon as the half-hour exam ended, Uston nervously asked Harrison for the verdict.

"To be honest," replied the man as he disconnected the electrodes, "I'd have to say I think Al's wasting his money on these polygraph tests."

A couple of days later Arnold Harrison called Francesco to report that all three Big Players had passed their lie detector tests. Although this news naturally came as a relief to Ken, Barry, and Steve, it frustrated Al, who was forced to abandon his search for the missing four grand. The following weekend he was still brooding over the loss at a special party Ken had thrown for his own birthday. The star attraction was Uston's idol, Erroll Garner, who entertained the entire team at the B.P.'s penthouse.

After accompanying the musician (who happened to be playing the Bay Area that week) on bass, Uston took a turn at the piano, playing several of the star's memorable compositions. During the refrain of one ballad, the Big Player lapsed into the double-time right-hand, guitar-like left-hand technique that Garner uses so effectively. The master was impressed.

"You should do the show for me tonight," he told Ken at the number's end.

After Garner finished up his final set with a "Misty" encore, he launched into a chorus of "Happy Birthday" with all twenty-one team members singing along. Then, just as the star walked out the door, $500 richer for his private performance, Judy marched in from the kitchen carrying a lit birthday cake with a king and ace iced onto the top. Ken tore open the accompanying card from the counters. It read: "Happy Birthday—You can count on us!"

While everyone was eating their cake Al pulled out a chart he had brought along and propped it up against the piano. The counters gathered around as he showed how the team could win $16,000 to $66,000 more per trip if they played faster, abandoned minus decks unlikely to turn hot, and made better use of relay signals for referring B.P.'s to hot tables.

When he finished Judy took the floor. Standing in front of Ken's picture window she told the players, "I've been with this team since the start. Originally, the B.P. got roughly triple a counter's share. That ratio has continually increased until now it's 6 to 1. For example, on our last trip each B.P. got 15 percent of the total bank while each counter got 2.5 percent. That seems too high to me; I think counters as a group should be entitled to 50 percent of the bank instead of 40 percent."

Before she had a chance to finish, Judy was cut off by Barry. "That's ridiculous. I've won over $100,000 for the team. Anyone who thinks they can do the job I've done, stick up their hand."

No arms were raised but Judy quickly replied, "I'm

not questioning your right to a larger proportion but I think you've got too much more than the counters."

"Goddammit," said Barry, "the 60–40 split is fair. We risk our lives carrying all that cash around. We're going to get barred someday and you counters can go on forever."

"The whole concept will be blown when the first B.P. is barred," said Judy. "We'll be out just like you."

"I disagree, but if there's any disparity in earnings, it's between the good counters and the less productive ones. You're all getting paid about the same and yet some of you contribute far more than others. For example, the equal split really isn't fair to Karen, who does such a terrific job."

"What do you mean?" shouted Judy. "I'm certainly as good as she is."

"So am I," yelled Barker, as the newer counters murmured to one another.

"Now wait just a goddam minute," said Barry. "How many of you honestly think you can count as well as anyone else on the team?"

When virtually all the counters' hands shot up, the B.P. said, "OK, OK, I'll tell you what. Since it's obvious you can't be objective about yourselves let's have the Big Players rate counter ability. That will give you a fair basis for reapportioning your 40 percent bank share."

After much discussion the counters agreed to Barry's proposal with the understanding that the maximum disparity would be 3 to 2. With this problem settled, Al proceeded to interrogate the B.P.'s about various complaints he had picked up from other players during the *Ocean's 11* trip. The majority of the time was spent on Ken, who was forced to defend himself against a wide range of charges.

"Ken, you took chances on casino pay phones, didn't you?"

"Right, Al, it was a mistake."

"You met Barry at the Landmark after he finished a session and had dinner with him in the coffee shop."

"Yes, and I won't do it again."

"It seems you were shortchanged on a payoff while showing off at the Sahara."

"Possibly."

"You played half as many hands as Barry or Steve."

"That's true."

"You took chances with Vegas girls."

"Not really."

"You missed one of our team meetings. I suppose you were with your hooker friend."

"I'm afraid so."

"You made ridiculous wasteful bets on minus decks. Four or five plays off the top would have allowed you to stay roughly even and been better cover."

"Sorry."

When the inquisition ended twenty minutes later, team members drifted out. One of the last to go was Francesco. After finishing off his cake, he walked to the elevator with his host.

"Hey, Al," asked Uston, "why did you come down so much harder on me than Steve or Barry?"

"Because you deserved it."

"Now come on. You know I'm not going to fight

you in front of the whole team. You know most of those things I did were justified. Sure I played less hands, but that was because I was being careful about cover. I bet minus decks because they were adjacent to tables where I'd just been shuffled on. By wheeling to bet the nearest available shoe I kept the flow going, convinced the bosses I wasn't counting, and avoided further casino countermeasures. What difference does it make if I may have been shortchanged $25 at the Sahara? The key thing was that by looking away from the table during payoffs I helped insure future play. And I wish you'd stop bugging me about Jean. I've told you she's an integral part of my high-roller act. Besides, I always put my money in the safe deposit box before taking her to my room."

"Ken, do you think that just because you're some big shot executive that you're above criticism?"

"Of course not. I get taken down plenty at the exchange."

"Well, then maybe you should sit down and start thinking more about the team's interest."

"How so?"

"Ken, you're greedy, you're selfish, and if you don't start watching yourself more carefully, you're going to wipe all of us out."

"Al, goddammit. Don't you understand it's all an act? I'm doing the Big Player role for the team's own good."

"I used to believe that," said Francesco as he walked onto the elevator, "but I don't think you're acting anymore."

"Al, come on."

"Night, Ken. Happy Birthday."

171.1235 *Gaming licensee may detain person suspected of having committed felony in gaming establishment.*

3. Detention pursuant to this section shall be in the establishment, in a reasonable manner, for a reasonable length of time and solely for the purpose of notifying a peace officer. Such taking into custody and detention shall not render the licensee or his officers, employees or agents criminally or civilly liable for false arrest, false imprisonment, slander or unlawful detention unless such taking into custody and detention are unreasonable under all the circumstances.

—*Proceedings to Commitment*
Nevada Revised Statutes

THE MEETING HAD GONE remarkably well. In a matter of hours Ken Uston persuaded the stock exchange managers to make the cuts necessary to wipe out the projected $600,000 deficit and balance the 1975 budget. Then, just prior to adjourning the session at the Marriott Hotel in Los Angeles, he asked for questions.

"Yes, I have one," said a depository official as he held up a document from the thick budget packet that Ken had passed out to everyone. "When are we getting to this memo about B.P.'s and counters?"

Uston smiled, walked over for a look, picked up the document, and then retrieved everyone else's copies, explaining, "Sorry guys, that's for another departmental meeting."

Looking over the memo on the plane back to San Francisco, Uston kept asking himself how he could have made such a disastrous mistake. Clearly his preoccupation with blackjack was overwhelming his exchange work. Still, it was one hell of a good memo:

To: Team Members
From: Ken
Subject: Suggestions for Improved
          Security and Higher Profits

1. Al will be in his room at predetermined hours, before, during and after a session.
   a. If B.P.'s need to contact counters, they will phone Al, who will in turn call the team captain.
   b. If counters need to reach B.P.'s, the team captain will call Al, who will contact the B.P.
2. All B.P.'s will have code names for casino paging. Barry will be Billy Mark, Steve will be Stuart Johnson, and Ken will be Ken Saunders.
3. The team will develop a third set of signals for future trips.
4. We will stagger starting times and not begin on the hour.

5. Counters should back away from basic strategy at the end of the deck to save cards for the B.P.
    a. No splitting if B.P. is playing, except ace–ace and 8–8 against small cards.
    b. Absolutely no *resplitting*.
6. Don't call in B.P. at the end of the deck if he can play only one spot.
7. Stay away from tables where other counters are playing.
8. If you call in a B.P. several times in a row at a given table and play head on with him, change to another table where there is at least one other nonteam player.
9. B.P. will move counters to different tables by rubbing his nose. Counters have consistently missed this signal. WATCH FOR NOSE SIGNAL.
10. Counters should minimize cracking $100 bills as much as possible.
11. No group air fares. Everybody makes own flight reservations and pays for own plane tickets.
12. Ask for businessmen's rate at motel. Say you work for some large company like IBM.
13. Counters should have a prearranged interrogation story as outlined by Al. Tell the truth. Give them your name, where you're from, and explain that you like blackjack. But don't go beyond that. You have nothing to worry about. Everything the team does is completely legal. The chances of being detained are slim. Probably the worst the clubs will do is shuffle up on us.

At 4:00 P.M. the following Thursday Uston sat in his office running through ace adjustment tests with the help of nineteen decks spread out over his desk, in and out boxes, plus a good portion of the floor. Halfway through the practice session he took a call. It was bad news:

"Several weeks earlier the exchange president had recommended that the board upgrade titles of a number of officers, including myself. Although our directors agreed to raise the title of several of my subordinates to senior vice-president, they refused to elevate me to executive vice-president. While the new title would not have meant a salary increase, I was concerned that by not stepping up a level I would have trouble enforcing budgets and programs under my direction. Worried about this, the president came up with an imaginative solution—he would rescind the other promotions. Unfortunately, the chairman had declined to ratify the move at a meeting that morning. I was no longer the exchange's only senior vice-president.

"From my experience in the business world I knew that the day you lost your upward mobility was the day to begin submitting resumés elsewhere. But there was no time for job interviews. Every spare moment was tied up with the team. After all, if we kept winning the way we'd done on *Ocean's 11*, I'd be independently wealthy within a year. And then I wouldn't have to worry about the stock exchange or any other executive hierarchy.

"Certainly the casinos were doing everything possible to facilitate my new avocation. Sitting on my desk that very afternoon was an invitation to play in the Sands' Sixth Annual Pro-Am Golf Tournament. Attached was a handwritten note from a Sands representative who had comped me a prestigious eighteenth-floor tower suite for the big event. 'On future trips,' he added in a postscript, 'please give your plane tickets to our cashier so we can refund your air fare.'

"I continued working with my nineteen decks until Al, dressed as always in his seedy black leather jacket, walked in and dropped his $64,000 cash contribution to the latest team bank in my lap. After pooling this money with my $19,000 share I stuffed all 830 of the $100 bills into a money belt he had loaned me. As we walked out of the office my secretary, Mary, looked at me suspiciously.

" 'What's wrong?' I asked.

" 'Well, it's just that you look so . . . so lumpy.'

" 'Whereabouts?'

" 'Around the middle.'

" 'You mean here,' I said, patting my midriff.

" 'Right.'

" 'Well maybe I should redistribute the wealth,' I said, unbuttoning my coat, slipping the money out of the belt and dividing it between various pockets.

" 'How's that, Mary?'

" 'OK. But I think you'd look better with a bodyguard.' "

Mary had little reason to worry. When Ken arrived in Las Vegas he was picked up at the airport by a Sands security guard, one of the many little favors the casino extended its valued guests. When he entered his commodious, one-bedroom suite, equipped with a private bar, he found a basket of fruit wrapped in green cellophane. Attached was a handwritten note from the manager: "We're delighted to have you back."

Except for the coffee shop waitress who refused to serve him a roll unless he sat down, Uston was pampered by every employee he dealt with. During one of many meals in the Regency Room, Stan Frederick came in to make sure everything was all right.

"It's fabulous," said Uston, who was then being pampered by four waiters plus the maître d'. "You know I'd like to lay some bread on you but I heard that tipping bosses is out. Maybe you could use a stereo or something. If I make some money, I'll take care of you."

"Thanks," whispered the pit boss, "you can always slip me something."

Uston promptly pushed a $100 bill into his hand saying, "Hey, look, if you hear anything I should know about, I'd appreciate your keeping me posted."

"Of course," said the pit boss.

Arriving in town ahead of Al and the other B.P.'s, Ken kicked off the trip with a $20,000 win at the Tropicana. Exhilarated by his performance, he phoned the good news home. Francesco and Barry were delighted but unfortunately Steve was out.

"When will he be back?" Uston asked the babysitter.

"About eleven, I think."

"Well, could you give him a message?"

"Sure."

"Just tell him Ken called and said he won $20,000 at the Trop."

Unfortunately, by the time Steve returned home that night Ken's win had been obliterated by a disastrous Sands session:

"I had started out playing against $44,000 in front money * on deposit in the Sands cage. In addition I had another $30,000 on deposit at the Tropicana. Losing steadily, I drew a series of $5,000 markers until finally Stan cut me off.

" 'What's wrong?' I asked.

" 'You used up all your front money.'

" 'No way. I've only lost $34,000. I've got another $10,000 left.'

"Stan walked over to the pit desk returning with a sheaf of markers. Leafing through them I saw that they totaled $44,000. After making sure none of them were counterfeit, I realized that under the pressure of playing I'd underestimated my loss by $10,000. Since the deck remained hot I appealed to Stan for more credit. 'Look, here's my receipt for $30,000 on deposit at the Trop. So give me another 5.'

" 'Sorry, Ken, I'd really like to help you, but they won't let me do it.'

" 'What do you mean they won't let you do it! I'm one of your best customers, I'm comped in your hotel, I've just given you guys $44,000 in the last three hours, and you won't give me a cent even though I've got thirty grand sitting five minutes away.

---

* Front money can be left with the cashier by a cash player. When a player wants chips to play with he writes a special casino check (known as a marker) against these funds.

I don't need to stand for this nonsense. I'm moving out.'

" 'Hey, Ken, relax. I'll go over to the Trop right now to pick up your money. As soon as I get back you can resume playing.'

"Although disappointed about being unable to play out my hot deck, as well as a superhot situation Barker had found at an adjacent table, I decided to take Stan up on his offer to play courier. A few minutes later Hank, who was managing the night shift at the Tropicana, called and I authorized the $30,000 withdrawal. After hanging up I realized it was a terrible mistake to let a Sands boss run errands for me at the Trop. No doubt Stan had a few words with Hank. Perhaps they compared notes on my peculiar table-hopping style.

"Anxious to unwind, I walked into the adjacent cocktail lounge, through the curtains surrounding the empty bandstand (it was now 4:00 A.M.), sat down at the piano, and began playing a little Erroll Garner. I was deep into 'Dreamy' when Stan, looking pleased to be my delivery boy, walked through the curtains and gave me a $30,000 Sands deposit receipt.

" 'Now admit it, Ken,' said the boss, as he finished handing over my cash, 'don't you feel better having all your money in one place?'

"When I returned to the pit all the Sands personnel pretended the entire fiscal crisis had never happened. To some extent I think their warmth was influenced by the fact that I continued losing steadily. After dropping another $1,500 I realized that with just a few more bad hands my deficit would total $50,000, nearly half the team bank. But despite the magnitude of my loss I forced myself to act unconcerned. 'You know,' I told one of the dealers after dropping $500, 'if this keeps up I'm going to be forced to sell an oil well.'

"It took considerable self-discipline for me to pretend that a $50,000 win or loss was inconsequential. Back when I'd first played Thorp on my own, a $100 win or loss was cause for either hollering in triumph or slamming the table in disgust. Now I would chew out the bosses for shuffling or credit problems, but I would never show emotion over playing results.

"In some ways I think this was probably the hardest part of being a B.P. When I won $27,000 in forty-five minutes I wanted the whole town to know it, and when I lost $44,000 in one session I wanted to go home. Standing there dropping thousands in full view of counters who had invested in me was bad enough. But to have other players standing around making cracks like 'If he keeps this up the Sands is going to be adding another Tower,' was the ultimate disgrace. There was nothing I could do except sip my milk to quell the sharp stomach pain that suddenly came over me."

Rallying in the final half hour, Ken managed to end the session with a $32,500 loss. Despite this dramatic dumping, assistant casino manager Herb Nunaz was anything but pleased with the Big Player's performance. Watching his plays, the Sands official began to understand the reason behind his table-hopping style—he had agents around the pit who counted down the decks. After studying Uston's action for about twenty minutes he was convinced that the high roller's helpers were bringing him in with the aid of hand signals.

A less experienced casino employee might have been tempted to throw Ken out on the spot. But not Herb Nunaz. He wanted more than the ringleader. He wanted to nail every single member of the team. After all, what value was there in banishing one scheming counter if his cohorts were simply going to rush back in with a new leader the following day? The Sands man proceeded to do the smart thing—he alerted pit boss Howard Rambicour and foreman Sam DeFrancesco. Then the three men kept careful track of each player working the tables where Uston played. As soon as they finished identifying the culprits, Nunaz would make his move.

Oblivious to this surveillance, Uston left the casino after arranging to see Stan Frederick the following day for lunch at the Mamchen Deli; he hoped to learn why the casino had been so uncooperative the previous night. But the Sands official, who was ignorant of Nunaz's surveillance of Uston, proved completely uninformative.

"What's the matter?" Ken asked. "Can't you tell me anything anymore?"

"It's not that. It's just that this isn't the best place to talk. Meet me tonight at 1:00 A.M. in the airport's main slot area."

Following Stan's instructions, Ken arrived at the appointed time and busied himself with a quarter machine. About fifteen minutes later his friend showed up, played a few rounds on an adjacent unit, and then whispered, "Follow me."

Clearing the security check, they proceeded through the deserted terminal to United Airlines' gate 54. "Sorry we had to come so far," apologized the pit boss. "I used to like the Western and Frontier lounges, but lately I've been finding United's are the quietest this time of night."

"You come out here often?"

"No, just when I get depressed."

"Depressed?"

"Right. I can look at all the destinations and think how lucky I am not to have to live in all those horrible places like New York, Denver, San Francisco, and Los Angeles. I mean people are always making fun of Las Vegas, but the fact is they're just jealous of everything we've got. Think about it, Ken. Las Vegas is the only city in the country that's actually fun to be in. People really have a good time here. The reason I don't take vacations is because there's no need to. Just living here is a perpetual holiday. Take you, for instance. Everyone's always talking about what a great place San Francisco is. But if it's so wonderful, what are you doing in Las Vegas all the time?"

"Good point. But why did you bring me all the way out here?"

"Because we can talk without being overheard. Now look, I know this is none of my business, Ken, but if you're comped at one casino it looks a little strange to have $30,000 on deposit at another club. See what I mean?"

"But I thought I had an A-1 player rating."

"You did, until one of the managers called your bank and found out you had under $1,000 on deposit."

"So what? Everyone lives on credit cards."

"I know that, but it still doesn't look good. Anyway, don't worry about it. What I really wanted to talk about was my trip over to the Tropicana yesterday. They were asking some very strange questions about you."

"Like what?"

"Well, they wanted to know why you'd left all that money with them when you were staying with us."

"What did you tell them?"

"I just said you appeared to be the sort of guy who liked a little variety."

"Did that satisfy them?"

"Oh, one of the pit bosses, I can't remember his name, said he thought you were using some kind of system. I told him that was crazy; that if anything, you were probably the most unsystematic player I'd ever seen. But they still seem suspicious. If I were you, Ken, I think I'd stay out of that place for a while. Stick with us; we'll take care of you."

The following morning Uston headed over to the Aladdin, where he handed over $30,000 in cash to Barry in the men's room. Now that the whole team was in town, Al had decided to try to recoup Ken's big loss by conducting a major offensive along the lines of the previously successful "Operation Hank" at the Tropicana. This time a team of ten counters moved in on the Aladdin's eight open tables while

Barry stood in the pit conducting operations like an orchestra leader. Every time he picked up a hot signal he dispatched another pit boss to place his bets.

Within half an hour Barry found himself playing as many as five tables simultaneously. Action was held up as the bosses shouted across the pit for instructions on whether to hit, stand, split, or double down on each hand. Because the pit was virtually deserted, club officials were perfectly happy to slow the play down to Barry's pace. This created an unusually favorable situation for the team. The B.P. was actually able to keep an average of three or four hands going at once. When pit bosses started to tire from running back and forth for chips, he decided to help them out by leaving stacks of $100 chips down on each table.

This astonishing show captured the interest of everyone in the club, from elderly bingo players to club manager Mel Hayes, who took a seat next to Karen, who was playing her real-life role as Barry's girl friend. Although she had been playing her table under the B.P.'s supervision, the counter was now forced to defer to the unsolicited advice of the Aladdin official. Not only did he push Karen into playing off the top of the deck, but he also encouraged her to bet anything she won on subsequent hands. Anxious not to offend Mel, she gradually began letting him handle all her table bets for Barry. But when the manager began spreading to two hands she nervously suggested that perhaps it was time to back off. Mel ignored her.

Instead of arguing further, Karen called Barry over

to the table to take out another marker. By the time he finished she had pocketed all her chips and ditched Mel by heading for the ladies' room. Despite these and other administrative problems, the B.P. still managed to play his way to a $6,000 victory. Inspired by this success, he returned the following day with ten other counters including Al, who had on his wig and goatee. Once again Barry orchestrated the play beautifully. The only problem was that he closed the session out with a $27,000 loss. But the dumping did not discourage him, convinced as he was that by putting such a huge volume into action the conductor concept would eventually yield a bonanza. Unfortunately, when he returned with his counters for a third session, a pit boss met him at the cage with bad news: "I'm really sorry, Barry, but Mel has passed the word he doesn't want you to play."

This did not help team morale. Although Aladdin bosses had not uncovered the team approach, they were obviously intimidated by Barry's unconventional style of play. If other clubs followed suit and started banishing B.P.'s from the pit after a big dumping, the team could be wiped out.

Barry's loss was compounded by several more disastrous sessions for Ken. By the end of his third day in Las Vegas, he was down a total of $81,500. Standing in line for the $3.95 all-you-can-eat brunch at the Caesar's Palace Circus Maximus showroom Sunday morning, he realized this sudden decline put his cumulative B.P. career deficit at $33,000. While within the realm of statistical probability, this loss rate was every bit as bad as Ron Reardon's.

Walking past the serving tables to pick up brittle blintzes, tiny sweet rolls, yo-yo-sized bagels, runny eggs, salty tea, and false-bottomed glasses of champagne, Uston wondered if this performance might not spark a move to demote him to counter status. He was so depressed that he hardly noticed the young man with a buffalo headdress rehearsing a dance on the Circus Maximus stage with a woman wearing a pink bikini and gold, feather-trimmed helmet.

As he finished brunch with Michelle, a Los Angeles friend who had joined him for a few days, Ken heard his name being paged. It was Al summoning him to a special team meeting at K.P.'s apartment. After dropping his friend off at the Sands, Uston rode out to meet with the assembled team. Al led him into the kitchen for a private talk. As soon as the door was closed Francesco started in on him:

"This has nothing to do with all the money you're losing, but some of the counters are critical of the way you're handling yourself. You were a half hour late for one session and fifteen minutes late for another. They didn't like seeing you let Michelle bet some of your money last night. One of our new counters, Harry Stone, claims you didn't notice him at the Sands. The guy got so mad he just walked out after an hour and a half. You also missed a lot of hot signals from K.P. and the other counters. Also, Barker claims he caught you doubling on an ace–9 against a deuce."

"I did the best job possible," said Uston. "I wasn't late for any sessions, I didn't make that ace–9 double down, and I don't even know what Harry Stone looks like. You've got to let me answer all these charges in front of the entire group."

When the two men entered K.P.'s living room Uston was surprised to find a number of counters supporting him:

"Karen patted me on the shoulder, Tony nodded sympathetically, and Barker voiced disbelief at the incredible number of bad hands I'd been dealt on hot decks: 'It was incredible, Ken; when you were at my table I won $150 betting nickles while you lost $10,000.' "

As Ken began to speak it was clear that the more statistically sophisticated counters understood that he wasn't incompetent or over-reporting losses dishonestly:

"They knew that I had simply been victimized by extreme negative swings. Several of them asked if I thought the Sands had been cheating. More than one counter had noticed that replacement decks weren't brand new. They thought that perhaps these cards had been preordered to the house's advantage. But I defended the Sands' integrity, explaining that I had taken gradual downward swings as opposed to a big dumping at one table. Although it was likely that a club might have one or two cheating dealers, it was improbable that all of them would be dishonest. Everyone bought this argument and agreed that since heavy losses had ingratiated me to the casino, I should continue playing there.

"After covering the Sands I began asking about some of the criticisms Al had told me about.

" 'Now who said he saw me double on ace–9 against a deuce?'

" 'I did,' said Barker. 'It was when you played with that drunken Texan who kept saying how you really had balls to bet so courageously.'

" 'Barker,' I replied, 'the dealer had a 5 up, not a 2, and the count was sky-high.'

" 'That's right,' shouted Gary Johnson, a new counter who had been standing in the small group that had gathered to watch my play. 'The dealer did have a 5.'

" 'OK,' I said, 'now who said I was late for a session?'

"It was Barker again: "You didn't show up until 12:45 for the session on Friday night.'

" 'That's impossible. I had a wake-up call for midnight and couldn't sleep. So I got up before the call, took a shower, and was in the casino a minute or two after the 12:15 starting time.'

" 'He's telling the truth,' said Tony. 'I assumed he was fifteen minutes late because I thought the session started at midnight.'

" 'No,' I explained, 'the counters were supposed to be there at midnight. The session was scheduled for 12:15 A.M., so at most I was a couple of minutes late. Now about this Harry Stone guy—I wouldn't know him if I ran into him.'

" 'He was at Al's house for our last meeting,' said Judy.

" 'Then why didn't anyone introduce me to him? There were all sorts of husbands and boyfriends of counters around that night. This illustrates one of the big problems with our expanded organization. We've lost communication. Everyone has to work on getting it back. Now, as far as these charges about missing hot decks. Sometimes I have to overlook some of you. Remember the Sands has a big L-shaped pit that makes it hard to get around the casino. If I don't see you, it's probably because you're at a crowded table and I don't want to risk blowing cover by running around the L. The last thing we want is to have bosses wondering why it's so important for me to get to a particular table on the other side.'

" 'Ken's right,' said Steve. 'It's really discouraging when you take a huge loss. I can tell you that from my own experience. He knows the numbers better than I do and plays blackjack as well as anyone in this town. I've got complete confidence in his ability as a B.P. It's important that we all let him know we still believe in him one hundred percent.'

"The room broke into applause and I actually found myself tearing up. While wiping my eyes with a Kleenex I could hear someone giving the coded team knock at the door. Al promptly opened up and ushered in a tall, dark-haired, mustachioed young man.

" 'Haven't I seen you somewhere before?' I asked while shaking hands with the new arrival.

" 'Could be.'

" 'Why you must be, uh . . .'

" 'Harry Stone, Ken, Harry Stone.' ' "

After the team meeting ended Ken ushered Barry, Steve, and Al into K.P.'s bedroom. Reviewing the disastrous experience of the past few days, he argued that it was time to reconsider buying Ed Saunders' mysterious new system. Although his teammates remained dubious, they agreed to meet with Saunders that night over dinner at Caesar's Bacchanal.

Doing business with Ed at the restaurant proved more difficult than the previous time because of his preoccupation with the vestal virgins. Calling them back repeatedly to rub his aching back, the blackjack expert continued his circular talk, ducking direct questions and telling parables. Finally the group reached the familiar impasse. Saunders wanted his money up front while Al insisted on a look at the system first. Totally frustrated, Ken jumped up. "All right, goddammit. I'll pay the $5,000. I trust Ed and think his system will work. If not, he'll give the money back. Now let's finish our dinner."

Al immediately tossed Ken a $5,000 packet. But Barry said, "Hey look, I trust Ed too but I think the probability of his having a better system is no higher than 10 percent."

"It really upsets me to see you fighting like this," Saunders interjected. "I really don't want to sell systems. I just like you guys and want to see you do better."

"Then let us try the system first," said Al. "Our credit is good, isn't it?"

"Say," Ed replied, "did I ever tell any of you the story about what the Bolivian Army did with Che Guevara's body after executing him?"

While the teammates continued bickering Saunders finished his dessert and then beckoned to one of the gold-uniformed vestal virgins. "Do you think you could rub over on the left just below my shoulder blade?"

"Here?" asked the waitress.

"No, a little lower."

"Here?"

"A little to the right."

"Here?"

"Perfect."

Unable to resolve their dispute the leaders finished eating and promised to call Ed with their decision in a few days. Back at the Sands, Ken told Michelle, his friend from L.A., about the dinner meeting. She was openly skeptical of Saunders. Deeply involved in parapsychology, she suggested that perhaps it would be appropriate for Ken to hold up play until he got some expert psychic advice.

"I don't really understand that ESP stuff," Uston told her.

"Maybe you'd be doing better if you did."

After listening to his young friend for half an hour, to amuse her, Ken agreed to take an extrasensory longshot to break out of his slump. The following morning they rode out to Larry Lee's Southwestern Temple of Spiritual Science, distinguished by a revolving sign that read: FAITH HEALING, ASTROLOGY, PALMISTRY, COSMIC CHANTS, TELEPATHY, TAROT, CRYSTAL BALLS, CONJURE BAGS, VOODOO, TALISMANS, DRIVE-IN FORTUNE TELLING. WE ACCEPT ALL MAJOR CREDIT CARDS.

"Have you ever been to this place before?" Ken whispered, as they walked into the Temple.

"No, but one of my friends came here last year and got some super pimpernel."

"What's that?"

"It's an herb, dummy. People use it to prevent accidents and illness."

Inside they were greeted by a gray-haired man wearing Adidas shoes, formal trousers, a tie-dyed dress shirt, and a yin-yang pendant that reached all the way down to his cummerbund. He looked tired.

"I suppose you're down on your luck and want to know if you should keep playing," Larry Lee said to Ken.

"How'd you guess?"

"Because that's just about all we ever get around here. It's ridiculous. I've gone to a lot of expense to give Las Vegas a first-class psychic center. And what thanks do I get. I've got ten pounds of ginseng root rotting in the backroom, no one will touch any of my fetish dolls, and I don't think I could even give my Lucifer rings away. All anyone wants is quickie fortune telling and a rabbit's foot. . . . Forgive me for taking the liberty of complaining to you people. It's just that I'm exhausted these days because I have to do everything myself. Things are so bad that I've had to lay off my assistant. Imagine that, one of the best faith healers in the West living on unemployment. And now the IRS is refusing to let me deduct the cost of teleporting myself to a psychic convention in Brazil."

After Ken commiserated with Larry Lee and handed him his $6.50, the two men entered the psychic's private office. Standing next to a table covered with a map of Las Vegas, the expert slowly went into a trance.

"Ken," he said, "do you see that Wishing Bag over on my desk?"

"The green one?"

"No, that's the Fixed-Nutmeg Bag. It's the one directly to the right."

"Got it."

"Open it up."

Following orders, Uston loosened the Wishing Bag's drawstring and pulled out a piece of parchment from amongst the Mojo Wishing Beans, the Job's Tears, and the Seal of Magic. Then he wrote down his secret wish on the parchment. When he finished, Larry Lee began rubbing his hands up and down the map of Las Vegas.

"Ken, I'm feeling very good about your prospects all of a sudden. I think I've found the casino where you can really win. Come over here and tell me where my finger is on the map."

"Nellis Air Force Base."

"Damn," said Larry Lee, "I knew I should have made you take the Fixed-Nutmeg Bag."

171.124 *Arrests by peace officers*

> 2. He [a peace officer] may . . . at night, without a warrant, arrest any person whom he has reasonable cause for believing to have committed a felony, and is justified in making the arrest, though it afterward appear that a felony has not been committed.
>
> —*Proceedings to Commitment*
> *Nevada Revised Statutes*

"GOOD MORNING, MR. USTON," said the Sands operator. "It's 10:30 and the temperature is sixty-seven degrees."

The Big Player rolled over and gave his Fixed-Nutmeg Bag a big squeeze. He didn't really believe that the road to gambling salvation lay through specially drilled nutmegs inlaid with quicksilver. Yet, as Ken said jokingly to Michelle, "At this point I'm willing to take all the help I can get." And, sure enough, the cards had finally turned in his favor. The 16s, 15s, and 14s that Ken had been getting suddenly changed to 20s, blackjacks, and 11 double downs. That night he set a new team record, winning $22,000 on one shoe.

Meanwhile, Barry had been dumping the Desert Inn. He later told Ken, "Man, what a session. All I ran into were superhot decks, so I spread the table—they had to break out the $1,000 baccarat chips for me. After about 2½ hours I had all kinds of chips in my pockets, so I went to the john to count up. Figured I was up around 50 grand. Hell, I was up $80,000. So, I thought, 'Let's go for 100.' I played another half hour and lost. Still, when I called off the session, I was $57,000 up."

This new record greatly impressed the Desert Inn bosses, who responded by banishing Barry from their blackjack tables. When he went to the cashier to check out, he learned his comp had been withdrawn. And the club actually refused to release his money on deposit in the cage until he paid the $714 room bill.

Although ecstatic over Barry's win, Al was very upset about losing the comp: "You should have insisted that they pay for the room. After all, they're the ones who offered you the comp in the first place."

"I know," said Barry, "but I didn't want to jeopardize the $57,000 win for a lousy $714."

Barry's victory and the wins by Steve and Ken wiped out the team's deficit and put the group in the black by $20,000. Although Uston and Steve had to return home to their jobs, Barry and Al decided to continue playing. The other two B.P.'s agreed to rejoin them the following weekend. Late for his flight, Uston checked out of his hotel in a rush. He returned fifteen minutes later.

"Back already?" asked Stan Frederick.

"I forgot something," explained Ken as he headed to the cage and took the $25,000 out of his safe deposit box.

As soon as Ken returned to San Francisco he began making plans for his return to Nevada. His work day was largely taken up with blackjack practice and calls from Al. Francesco was now reluctant to let the team make any major strategy decisions without first consulting Uston. Walking through the exchange floor, looking at all the specialists scurrying around, Ken was forced to admit that his job had become little more than a periodic interlude to his Las Vegas avocation. Once he had loved watching the ticker tape flash all the latest quotations on his investments. But there was no excitement in that anymore. Of course, one could make a lot of money playing the market—but it was such a dull form of gambling. In Las Vegas the Big Player enjoyed respect, attention, and unlimited complimentary privileges everywhere he went. In the securities industry the important client got a free calendar from his broker every year.

On Friday evening Ken boarded his Nevada-bound flight with Steve, his wife, and several counters. Uston had hoped to leave earlier in the afternoon, but unfortunately, Barker, who was scheduled to work Ken's first session, held things up because he had to pick up his unemployment check. He was one of several jobless counters who complicated team scheduling, frequently joining trips late or leaving early to pick up their unemployment checks at the appointed time.

At the Las Vegas airport the group was met by Al

and Barry, who led the two Big Players into a men's room. Taking a stall adjacent to Ken's, Al slipped $50,000 in playing money to him under the partition; Barry and Steve followed suit. With the cash distribution completed, the men headed over to K.P.'s apartment for a B.P. meeting. Although the team was already down $11,000 for this extended trip, the main subject of concern was increasingly difficult playing conditions. In addition to being barred at the Aladdin and the Desert Inn, Barry found that all the downtown clubs were shuffling on him. Moreover, he was encountering new hostility at the MGM from a diminutive pit boss named John Wilson, whom the team derisively referred to as "the Eye in the Rug."

"Listen," Barry told his fellow B.P.'s, "we've really got to start watching it. Don't split 10s anymore. That's why I got barred at the Aladdin. It's too obvious; the smart pit bosses realize it's a good play."

"I don't know," Ken said, "the Sands bosses all think I'm crazy to split 10s. It's such a good way to get more money on the table."

"It's not worth the risk. You'll still have all those 10s in there for the next hand, and the play doesn't gain you that much."

"How about compromising," suggested Al. "Let's split 10s only when the count is sky-high, way beyond the necessary true count."

The leaders bought this idea, as well as Francesco's proposal to split only once. Thus if a 10 was dealt on a split 10, they would not split the hand again. This disappointed Ken, because some of his most dramatic wins had come from repeated splitting of 10s.

After the meeting Ken taxied over to the receptive Sands, where an apologetic clerk explained that the free tower suite they had promised was unavailable: "But we do have a nice suite with wet bar on the first floor which you can get to without going outside. It even has sliding glass doors that open onto the pool. All our junket directors prefer this type of room."

As soon as the bellman dropped off his luggage, the Big Player began taking countermeasures. First he put his book filled with blackjack fallacies out on the dresser. Next he slipped the $5,000 wrappers off the cash Al had given him and set them afire—that way the Sands people would have no way of knowing that the money came from the DI, Caesar's, the MGM, and the other clubs the team was playing. Then he poured some of the complimentary Scotch into glasses and down the toilet so that potential snoops would think he'd been partying.

Returning to the casino Ken deposited $30,000 at the cage and left the other $20,000 in a safe deposit box. Out in the pit he found conditions ideal. Several dealers stood with arms crossed behind open tables with four decks of cards invitingly fanned out over the green felt. Uston played even with the house for about an hour, spending the lulls between hot decks snapping his fingers, tapping his feet, and dancing to a first-rate jazz trio in the cocktail lounge facing the pit. After calling a break he hopped up on the bandstand to compliment Joe Eddy, the piano player. As the musician nodded his thanks Ken said, "Hey, how about letting me do a chorus? I play piano in San Francisco."

"Money talks."

"What key are you in?" asked the B.P., as he laid a $100 chip on top of the piano.

"F."

Ken sat down on the bench and yelled out to the pit, "Hey Stan, this one's for you." He played the last five choruses of a blues number as Joe clapped his hands and cheered the guest artist on. When Uston finished his long Garneresque tag, pit bosses, dealers, and players applauded as play in the 21 pit virtually stopped—no doubt a Las Vegas first.

The Big Player returned to the tables for another hour before calling off the session a respectable $3,500 ahead. As he cashed out, Michelle, who had just flown in for the weekend, arrived at the casino. After taking her to his room, Uston called Barry, Steve, and Al to invite them over for a drink. The B.P.'s agreed to come right over, but Al was against the whole idea. He took the phone from Steve and told Ken, "You know I don't approve of everyone getting together like that. Besides, I think you've been spending too much time at the Sands. You should play another club."

"Relax. They love my action here. There isn't anything they won't do for me."

"You're underestimating them, Ken. That was my mistake."

When Uston returned to the Sands casino the following evening, a pit boss picked up the phone and alerted Herb Nunaz that the Big Player was back. The assistant casino manager headed over to the pit, where he watched Uston play according to signals delivered by five counters he had worked with during previous sessions. The whole thing was becoming more and more obvious. As soon as one of his friends raised a hand to his chin, Uston would move in to bet the favorable deck.

Certain that he had uncovered both the system and the people who were perpetrating it, Herb Nunaz began closing in. First he had one of the pit bosses instruct a dealer to shuffle up on Uston. The Big Player left the table, walked over to table two, and signaled to a woman wearing a yellow pantsuit who had already been pinpointed as a member of the Uston team; then he went over to table one and signaled to a tall girl in a green dress who was also known to be part of the operation.

The assistant casino manager continued watching as Uston picked up a cup of coffee and headed over to table sixteen. There the Big Player signaled a dark-haired man sitting at third base by tapping his chest. When the player failed to get the message Ken repeated the gesture so desperately that coffee sloshed over the edge of his cup. Finally, the man began to head for the door. But before he could get away Nunaz dispatched a security agent to apprehend him and escort him to a back office. Then he walked over to the cage and told the cashier, "Put a freeze on Mr. Uston's money, and don't give him any more markers."

Although Ken was alarmed by Tony's apprehension, he decided the best cover would be to continue playing as if everything were normal. But when he asked the dealer for a $5,000 marker after losing several big hands, one of the pit bosses shook his head and told Ken he had to get them from the cage. Uston was furious:

" 'What do you mean?' I asked, anxious to play out the hot deck. 'I've got $30,000 in there.'

" 'You've got to go to the cage.'

"When my protest failed I rushed over to the cage to pick up the new chips necessary to take advantage of the favorable decks. Herb Nunaz, the friendly assistant manager who had comped many shows and dinners for me in the past was there waiting for me.

" 'Herb,' I asked, 'what's happening? I need more money.'

" 'Ken, come on in the office for a minute, will you?'

" 'Sure.'

"I followed him into the security guard's inner office, which had been made available to me in the past for counting cash. Herb went behind the desk while an informally dressed man in his middle thirties asked, 'What do you know about the count?'

" 'What are you talking about?'

" 'You know, the count.'

" 'Hey, I count aces as 1 and 11. I read a book by a guy named Thorp once but it was too complicated. I know some people can keep track of cards, but I . . .'

" 'Come on, Ken. Do you know anybody else here?'

" 'Yeah, I know Stan Frederick.'

" 'I don't mean anyone who works here. You know anyone else?'

" 'No. Well, yes, I know Joe the piano player. Nice guy.'

" 'You know anyone else here?' asked Herb Nunaz.

" 'No.'

" 'Wait here,' said the shift manager as he walked back into the casino. Ignoring his instructions, I strolled into the outer office, thinking about heading to the bar for a drink.

" 'Stay here,' said the man who had started the interrogation.

"Seconds after I returned to the inner office a security guard ushered Barker in to join me.

" 'Do you know him?' asked Herb, eyeing me suspiciously.

" 'No.'

" 'You've never seen him before?'

" 'No, never.'

Then the interrogator took out pencil and paper.

" 'Name?'

" 'Ken Uston.'

" 'Where do you live?'

" 'I have apartments in San Francisco and New York.'

" 'Come on, what's your address?'

"When I gave him San Francisco and New York addresses he refused to put them down. Instead he asked, 'If your mother were going to write you, where would she write?'

" 'The San Francisco address. Now would you mind telling me who you are?'

" 'Police. Who did you think we were? Where do you work?'

" 'The Pacific Stock Exchange.'

" 'What do you do there?'

" 'I'm a senior vice-president.'

" 'Do you have any identification?'

" 'Not on me, but I've got my driver's license and all kinds of other ID in my suite.'

" 'I don't know how you do it in California, but here you've got to have ID. Without it, it's a misdemeanor charge.'

" 'Hey, it's in my room. If you want, I'll get it.'

" 'You have to have it on you.'

" 'It's in this hotel. Besides, they know who I am out there.'

" 'Having ID in your room is just like having it in your house. It's not on you and you can be arrested.'

" 'I'm sorry. At first I didn't realize you were with the police.'

" 'Yes you did. Your attitude is lousy. You can be arrested. In fact, consider yourself arrested.'

" 'Wait. I do have my front-money receipt.'

" 'That's no good. Also it's done. You could give me all kinds of ID now, but you've already been arrested so it wouldn't mean a thing.'

" 'I haven't done anything illegal. I have no police record.'

" 'Tough.'

"Just then my name was paged over the Sands P.A. system. 'Look,' I said, 'would you let me take that call? It may be important.'

" 'OK, but don't say anything. Just tell them you'll be detained awhile.'

"Picking up the receiver I listened to Stan Frederick explain that I had just stood him up for a lunch date at the Mamchen.

" 'Sorry,' I told him, 'but I'm in some trouble here. They say I should tell you I'll be detained awhile. But I might need bail money or something. Talk to you later.'

" 'OK, Ken. Call if you need help.'

"Turning to the cop I said, 'That was one of the Sands' pit bosses. We were going to have lunch. These guys know me here. What's this all about?'

" 'I don't know.'

"Just then another security guard brought in Tony. Although Tony had been in the casino, he had not counted for me during the session. The interrogator sat him down, ordered me into the outer office, and closed the door. While the Sands bosses and police cross-examined Tony, I looked at Barker, who gave me a wink. A minute later Herb Nunaz came out of the inner office to tell one of the guards, 'There was a tall girl in a green dress and a blond woman wearing a yellow pantsuit, but they split.' He was obviously referring to Karen and K.P. Now I knew the Sands was definitely on to all of us.

"While we sat there silently, another man was brought in for passing a bogus cashier's check. Tugging at his handcuffs he asked me, 'How do we know these guys are cops? They didn't show me a badge.' Realizing I hadn't seen a badge either, I turned to Barker, addressing him like a stranger.

" 'Did they show you any ID?'

" 'Yes.'

"Next Judy was escorted in by yet another guard.

Like Tony, she had not counted for me during the session. Following her in were three long-haired young men with beards. I guessed they were plainclothesmen.

" 'Who are you?' Judy asked one of the cops.

" 'Police.'

" 'Where's your ID?'

"The cop showed her his badge but she wasn't satisfied. 'I didn't see it close enough.'

" 'Sit down or you'll get handcuffs like that guy over there.'

"Then the cop turned to a plainclothesman saying, 'They won't admit they know each other.'

" 'Typical.'

"It was ten more minutes before Tony emerged from the interrogation with a security man who took his picture and then said, 'Hit the front door.'

"As soon as he left Herb Nunaz turned to me saying, 'Ken, we want you out of here right away.'

" 'Sure, I'll pack up and be out in fifteen minutes. Hell, if you don't want my action, I'll go play somewhere else. It doesn't matter.'

"Then Eddie, the guard who had obligingly bounced the woman who hustled me several weeks earlier, read a trespass statute from a card warning that returning to the Sands would make me subject to arrest.

" 'And that applies to all Hughes hotels,' added one of the cops.

"Next a security man asked me to pose for a Polaroid snapshot. I took my glasses off and intentionally distorted my face as much as possible. After that one of the policemen led me into the inner office to be frisked.

"When they finally released me, I returned to my room, packed up, and walked out to the cage with my suitcase and unopened basket of apples, pears, and oranges. 'Thanks,' I told Herb while putting the gift down on the counter, 'I appreciate the fruit.' As he shrugged I tore off the note and read it to him.

" 'Welcome to the Sands. We hope your stay will be pleasant and appreciate your being with us.'

" 'Ken, we know what you're doing.'

" 'Come on, Herb, look at the bright side. You won $5,000 from me this morning.'

"After picking up my $45,000 in the cage and the safe deposit box, I stuffed the packs of $100 bills in various pockets. Then I handed a $20 bill to the security chief, telling him, 'I'd appreciate it if one of your men would drive me to the airport—I don't like carrying around all this cash.'

" 'No problem,' he said, summoning Eddie."

Fifteen minutes later Ken and his sentry rode the moving walkway through the air terminal listening to the imaginative P.A. announcements:

"Hi folks, Doc Severinsen here asking you to please stand to the right because Ed McMahon is about to crawl by on your left. . . . This is Anthony Newley. When approaching the end of the moving walkway, please watch your step. Totie Fields didn't and she wound up with a voice like Wayne Newton. . . . Hi, this is Dan Rowan. Please stand to the right and pass on the left. Unless you're a midget of course. Then you can go right underneath. Hello, Jerry Vale here. When approaching the end of the walkway watch your step, because when you get there I'll be selling my albums. . . ."

"Hey," said Eddie, as they stepped off the ramp and began walking the final hundred yards to Ken's plane, "I don't see Jerry Vale."

"No big loss," replied the Big Player.

"You're right, Mr. Uston. To tell you the truth I never did think much of 'Volare.' "

Several weeks later Ken met Al and Barry for drinks at Henry's Fashion. After bailing Barker out of jail for failing to have an ID at the Sands (a charge that was subsequently dropped), the rest of the players promptly followed Ken out of town. Because the Sands security had figured out the entire system, including hand signals, everyone agreed that the group would have to disband. While brokenhearted about the untimely death of his team, Francesco was proud to point out that his operation had set a record. Over the past year their blackjack winnings totaled $400,000 in Las Vegas and $200,000 abroad.

As Al and Barry described plans to resume playing on their own in France and the Caribbean, a waitress came over to take their orders.

"Scotch on the rocks," said Al.

"Coors," said Barry.

"Grapefruit juice," said Ken.

"Are you on the wagon or something?" Barry asked Uston after the waitress had left.

"Doctor's orders," he explained. "It doesn't mix with the penicillin he's got me on."

"Penicillin?"

"Yeah, I seem to have picked up a social disease."

Just then the waitress returned with the drinks. As Uston took a swig of his grapefruit juice, Francesco started laughing into his Scotch. "Well, Ken, I guess you're really *really* out of it now. You can't drink, you can't screw, and you can't play blackjack."

EPILOGUE

THE SANDS BUST did not end team play for Al, Ken, Barry, Steve, and a number of counters. After playing northern Nevada, France, South America, and the Orient, the blackjack entrepreneurs returned to Las Vegas. Although they were barred from a number of clubs, the players were always able to find a four-deck house that welcomed their business.

In part this was due to the use of disguises, mini-teams, and new counters who alternated with veterans like Barker, Karen, and K.P. But a key factor was Uston's decision to begin filing federal court suits against clubs that banned him from playing blackjack because he was too good at it. Claiming violation of the public accommodations law and of his civil rights, the Big Player filed Nevada cases in April 1975 against the Sands and the Dunes. Shortly thereafter, Ken resigned from the Pacific Stock Exchange to devote himself full-time to gambling and to the lawsuits.

Although Uston's decision to quit the securities world to pursue his litigation on behalf of card counters everywhere made the front pages across the country, a number of casinos failed to get the message. Accordingly, similar California cases were filed against the MGM, the Flamingo Hilton, the Holiday, and the Marina in December 1975 and in 1976. These California suits were subsequently dismissed because the court felt it lacked jurisdiction over the Las Vegas operations. Uston refiled them in Nevada federal court during June 1976, adding the Las Vegas Hilton and Silver City to the list.

News of Ken Uston's quest for $85 million damages from the eight clubs was carried nationally by the wire services. Soon reporters from such disparate media as the *New York Times, Hustler,* the *Wall Street Journal, Midnight,* and the Boston *Globe* were at his door. The San Francisco *Examiner* made Uston's cases their lead story in their New Year's Eve issue, playing him over such competition as Gulf Oil's secret cash payments to Senator Hugh Scott and a bombing at the Berkeley branch of the Bank of America.

A number of Las Vegas clubs remained receptive to Uston and his fellow Big Players. Although Ken, Steve, and Barry worked with smaller groups, they continued to win consistently. All three men were comped to lavish rooms in leading hotels on the Strip. While Uston lived for free in a $230-a-day suite at Caesar's, Steve and Barry stayed for nothing at the nearby MGM.

By June 1976 the Big Players and Al, who concentrated on French clubs, had collectively won over $1 million with the team concept. Impressed by this unprecedented achievement, a number of their friends began asking to be cut in on the team. As a result, that summer as many as three completely separate counting teams could be found working in Nevada on a given weekend. Barry was consistently the big winner, taking home enough money to buy several new apartment houses and a Mark IV. Tired of driving to the San Francisco airport, he also bought a twin-engine plane and hired a pilot who flew him from a neighborhood airfield to Las Vegas. Despite these purchases, much of his $250,000 winnings remained unspent. These funds were stored in a $760 home floor vault that he bought from Barker, who had started selling safes.

While Steve's win was half that of Barry's it was more than enough for him to buy an apartment house and move along toward his dream of fiscal self-sufficiency. Uston preferred retaining his profits so that he would have a playing reserve sufficient to weather negative swings. Al Francesco also held on to the bulk of his winnings, after splurging on a $90,000 house. By the summer of 1976 he had cut back on his blackjack, leading a semiretired existence around the tennis courts and pools of San Francisco. Periodically he would write another letter to his Paris lawyer about the Dieppe casino's unpaid debt. The former owner had promised a three-year payoff, but he had only come up with $900 by the summer of 1976. The collection was complicated by the fact that Francesco and the attorney did not read or write each other's language.

Although a number of counters continued playing Las Vegas with mini-teams, their profits merely supplemented their regular incomes. K.P. left Nevada for a restaurant job in San Francisco to be closer to Al. Karen kept on modeling. After divorcing Tony because of his infidelity, Judy got a job as a secretary. Although the lawyer was devastated by his second marital breakup, he gradually developed a philosophical attitude toward the whole thing. "I'm not saying you need to go through a couple of divorces of your own to be a good divorce lawyer," he told Ken one day, "but it sure doesn't hurt."

While some of the old counters returned to straight jobs, Ken organized a new team of his own and continued playing in Las Vegas. His fame as the most colorful high roller to hit Vegas spread nationwide as newspapers and magazines discovered he was good copy. In June 1976 the Sunday *New York Times Magazine* published a feature article on the Big Player; its cover, often reserved for presidential candidates in this election year, depicted him placing his $1,000 bets at the blackjack table. The October issue of *Playboy* also printed his photograph before turning its attention in the following issue to Jimmy Carter. When asked whether all the publicity would restrict his freedom to play, Ken replied:

"There are plenty of clubs abroad where money can be made—Walker Hill in Korea, Macao, London, France, and Egypt, just to name a few. As for Las Vegas, I'm optimistic that the lawsuits will establish a precedent. How can the courts allow casinos to offer a game of skill to the public and arbitrarily bar those they think are too skillful? I've been invited to speak at the 1976 National Gambling Conference, and I hope to make this point loud and clear."

As Uston's cases moved closer to trial, the gambling

press devoted an increasing amount of space to the litigation. The leading international gambler's newsletter, *Rouge et Noir*, offered to sell readers copies of depositions from the Dunes case for $6. In one exclusive interview this publication quoted a ranking Las Vegas casino executive's belief that Ken's litigation represented the number one threat to the future of Nevada's gambling industry. He pointed out that if Uston could get the courts to sanction card counting, many clubs would be in financial jeopardy.

This fact was not lost on many of the Big Player's friends and family, who worried openly about his determination to take extended Las Vegas gambling trips. They suggested Ken would be wise to stay out of town until the cases had been tried. One afternoon, after his mother had phoned him at Caesar's, pleading with him to leave the casino ("There's those mobsters in the casinos and they go boom, boom. I don't like it, Kenny."), he decided to call Al for advice on his personal security.

"Relax," the founder said. "There's no way anyone is going to touch you. The people worrying about you have been seeing too many movies. Things just don't work that way down there anymore. Take it from me."

"Thanks, Al. I really appreciate your saying that."

"Glad to help, Ken. Of course, my brother Angelo doesn't think you're going to live through the weekend."

 **aPPenDIX**

RULES OF THE GAME

It is essential that the successful blackjack player have a complete and totally accurate knowledge of the rules of the game. This section sets forth the rules used by most Las Vegas casinos. Variations in these rules and their advantage or disadvantage to the player are covered in Tables 1 and 2.

Players. Blackjack is played by a dealer, who works for the house, and from one to six or seven players.

Cards. In Las Vegas, many clubs offer four-deck games, using four standard 52-card decks dealt from a shoe. Some Vegas clubs use only two standard decks, and most casinos in northern Nevada, as well as some in Las Vegas, use only one standard deck, dealt by hand.

Largely as a result of Ed Thorp's innovative book on card counting, the Vegas casinos converted to four-deck shoes in order to make card counting more difficult. (It has also been shown statistically that the use of multiple decks increases the house advantage.) In 1975 and 1976 several clubs, including the Hacienda, Union Plaza, and Las Vegas Club, introduced the use of five, six, and even seven decks.

Value of Cards. Each card has the same value as its spot except for the ace and the picture cards. All picture cards are counted as 10; the ace can be counted as either 1 or 11 at the option of the player. A hand containing an ace that can be counted either as a 1 or 11 (that is, by counting the ace as 11, the hand does not exceed 21) is called a "soft" hand; all other hands are referred to as "hard" hands.

Object of the Player. To obtain a total greater than that of the dealer, but not higher than 21.

Naturals, or Blackjacks. If the first two cards dealt to a player are an ace and a 10, the player has a natural (a blackjack) and receives one-and-one-half times his original bet if the dealer does not also have a natural. On the other hand, if the dealer has a natural and the player does not, the player loses the total of his original bet. If both the dealer and the player have blackjacks, the hand is considered a tie.

Hitting or Standing. If the dealer draws a blackjack, the hand is settled immediately. In all other cases the player has the option of drawing additional cards, or "hitting." If the player wants an additional card, typical practice is for him to scratch the surface of the felt with his cards, indicating to the dealer that he wants a "hit." A player may draw as many cards as he wants, as long as his total is under 21. When the player elects to stand—that is, draw no additional cards—he tucks his first two cards under his bet in the spot before him.

Busting. If the player's cards exceed a total of 21, he has "busted" and loses the hand regardless of the dealer's total. Typically, when the player busts he throws his cards in, face up, and the dealer gathers them in and collects the player's bet. If the dealer busts, all players who have not busted win the hand from the house.

The Deal.   Each player is dealt two cards, both either face up or face down, depending on the rules of the house. The dealer also receives two cards, one face down and one face up. The dealer's card that is face up is referred to as the "up-card," and the value of this card is a key piece of information in determining playing strategy. The dealer's face-down card is called the "hole card." Additional cards dealt to the player are dealt face up, one at a time.

If the player and the dealer have the same total, and this same total is 21 or under, the hand is a tie, or a "push." No money settlement takes place and the dealer collects the player's cards. Typically, to indicate a tie to the player the dealer taps the table several times with his knuckles or with the cards that he has picked up.

Dealer's Play.   The dealer must draw cards until he has a total of 17 or above. In most Las Vegas clubs, if he has a soft 17 (for example, an ace and a 6), he must also stand. In some downtown Las Vegas clubs and in the northern Nevada clubs, the dealer must hit a soft 17, which provides the house with an additional advantage.

Doubling Down.   In most Vegas casinos a player may double the amount of his bet after looking at his first two cards and turning them over (face up); he can then receive only one additional card. The third card is dealt face down. Most casinos in northern Nevada allow doubling down only on hard totals of 10 or 11, thereby providing an additional advantage to the house.

Splitting Pairs.   If the player's two cards are identical in value, the player may "split" them by betting an amount equal to his original bet on the second card. He then draws additional cards on each of the split pairs, playing each hand (from his right to his left) in turn. If the player receives an additional card of the same denomination, he may continue to split. Most clubs will permit splitting pairs three times, for a total of four hands played, although some clubs allow splitting indefinitely—on one occasion at the Sands Hotel, where I was betting $1,000 per hand, I split 10s a total of eight times. (Face cards and 10s are considered as pairs, and may be split. However, in one club in Reno, the Nevada Club, and in France generally, the "tens" must be identical; for example, two jacks may be split, but a jack and a queen may not.)

If aces are split, a player may draw only one additional card on each ace, dealt face down. In all other cases, he may continue to draw as many additional cards as he wants, assuming he doesn't exceed a total of 21. If the player busts on any of his split hands, the dealer immediately picks up the busted hand and collects the bet.

Insurance. If the dealer's up-card is an ace, the player may make a side bet, referred to as "insurance." The amount of the side bet may equal one half of the player's original bet. If the dealer has a blackjack, the casino will pay the player 2 to 1 on his insurance bet. If the dealer does not have a blackjack, he collects the insurance bet. The bet is referred to as "insurance" since, if the dealer has a blackjack and the player does not, the insurance bet effectively has "saved" the player's original bet and there is no money settlement (the player has lost his original bet but has won an equal amount from his insurance bet).

Some of the casinos in northern Nevada, such as the Cal Neva Club and the Ponderosa, do not allow the insurance bet; English casinos allow insurance only when the player has a blackjack.

Under normal circumstances, the insurance bet is a poor bet for the player. There are times when the deck is rich in 10s that insurance should be taken, but only a card counter would be aware of these situations. For a counter, insurance can be particularly valuable, since the player has a favorable edge on the insurance bets at precisely those times when he has placed larger bets, that is, when the deck is rich in 10s.

Burning a Card. It is traditional in most single-deck, double-deck, and four-deck games for the dealer to "burn" one card, the first card of the new deal. The first card is placed in the discard pile, if there is one. If there is no discard pile (and generally there is not for single-deck games), the card is slid around to the bottom of the deck, face up, so that it hides the face of the bottom card of the deck from the players at the table. The experienced blackjack player should try to spot the value of this "burned" card and include it in his count. It is sometimes possible to see the bottom card as well. So, in a single-deck game, if you can see both cards you know the content of 1/26 of the deck before the deal has even begun.

Betting Limits. In most major Las Vegas clubs the betting limits are either $2,000 (MGM), $1,000 (Tropicana, Sands, Desert Inn), or $500 (Fremont, Mint). Privileged high rollers are allowed to bet as much as $3,000 per hand at Caesar's Palace, but the normal limit is $1,000. In some of the smaller clubs and downtown clubs and at some tables in the major clubs in northern Nevada, the limit is below $500. The limit can be circumvented quite easily, however, merely by placing more than one bet. In highly favorable situations, I have been able to bet as much as $7,000, simply by placing $1,000 at every spot on the table. The most money I ever had on the table for one deal was $12,000 at the $1,000-limit Sands Hotel. On another occasion, I bet $6,000 at the $500-limit Fremont Hotel, expanding the amounts bet on the original seven spots through doubling down and splitting and resplitting pairs.

Shuffling. In a single-deck game, shuffling is normally left to the option of the dealer. In many clubs the practice is to shuffle after approximately two thirds of the deck has been depleted; this is generally the practice at Harrah's in both Tahoe and Reno and at Circus Circus and the Las Vegas Hilton. However, some clubs, despite the proliferation of card counters, deal all the way down to the bottom of the deck, notably the Nevada Club in Reno.

In two-deck games, shuffling can either be at the immediate option of the dealer, or can be previously determined by the dealer placing a "joker," or plain-colored card, somewhere near the bottom of the deck. When this card is reached, the dealer will either continue the hand that is in progress and then shuffle the deck or shuffle immediately and then complete the round (as at the Riviera and Aladdin).

In four-deck games, the joker is generally placed about one-half of a deck up from the bottom. However, some clubs, when their bosses suspect counters, will move the joker up. In fact, I have seen the joker up as high as two decks, sealing off 104 cards from play. In some clubs, when card counting is suspected all the cards are pulled out of the shoe, regardless of where the joker is, and reshuffled. At one hand at the Stardust, where I had placed two $500 bets, the dealer pulled out three and a half decks from the shoe and shuffled up!

New Decks. Periodically the house will replace the cards in play with a new deck. This practice has become far more prevalent at Harrah's Tahoe, which was "stung" heavily through the insertion of marked cards. Pit bosses will generally collect the cards and sort them out to ensure that all the cards are there. In addition, they will inspect the deck carefully to make sure that the player has not crimped or otherwise marked the cards for his own purposes. In four-deck games cards are replaced less frequently, since each card gets less use in a given time span. When the cards are replaced, the clubs are required, according to gaming regulations, to bring in four new decks to ensure that all the cards are included. At the Sands, however, I have noticed that occasionally the decks were not replaced with brand new cards out of a sealed pack. This of course is a questionable practice, since the player has no way of being certain that four complete decks are being put into play unless he witnesses the opening of the new packs. There is the possibility, too, that when new cards are brought into play, the house advantage can be increased through inadequate shuffling of the new deck, which results in clumping of identical cards.

RULE VARIATIONS

THERE ARE A surprising number of rule variations in Nevada and foreign casinos. The primary ones are described below.

Doubling Down Only on Hard Totals of 10 or 11. This rule is nearly universal in northern Nevada. Basing his findings on computer analyses, Thorp indicated that the ban on doubling on a hard 9 costs the player .14 percent, that the ban on doubling on all soft hands also costs the player .14 percent; and that the ban on hard hands other than 9 costs the player almost nothing. Thus the total effect of this rule is to favor the house by roughly .28 percent.

Dealer Must Hit Soft 17. This rule, which favors the house by .2 percent, is also nearly universal in northern Nevada and downtown Las Vegas. In these areas, therefore, the player can generally assume that he is playing at a .5 percent greater disadvantage than in the major Las Vegas casinos (.28 percent loss because of restrictions on doubling down and .2 percent loss because of the dealer's requirement to hit soft 17).

Player May Double Down on Split Pairs. This rule is best demonstrated by an example. Assume that you have been dealt two 9s against the dealer's 5 and decide to split the 9s. On both 9s you are dealt a 2, giving you two hard totals of 11. A few clubs will allow you to double down on each of these hands, and this variation is referred to as "doubling down on split pairs." This practice is permitted currently by Caesar's Palace, the MGM, the Landmark, and the Frontier. Computer analysis reveals that this option is worth .13 percent to the player.

Surrender. The only other major rule variation in Las Vegas is the surrender option, which is currently offered at Caesar's Palace, the Thunderbird, the Riviera, and the Dunes. The surrender option permits the player to throw in his hand and give up one half of the amount he has bet, retaining the other half. This may be done only on his first two cards and only after it has been determined that the dealer does not have a blackjack.

The value of surrender to the player depends to a large measure on whether the player is using the count to vary his surrender strategy and the size of his bets. For the noncounting basic strategy player, surrender is probably worth .1 percent. Julian Braun, who devised a system called Hi-Opt, estimated that the surrender option benefits the player by .25 percent if the player is using a 1-to-4 bet ratio and playing proper surrender strategy.

Effect of Rule Variations. The effect of rule variations on the player is summarized in tables 1 and 2. In general, the basic strategy player (single-deck) will be playing at about a .5 percent disadvantage in the northern Nevada clubs, .2 percent disadvantage at the downtown Las Vegas clubs, and about even with the house in major Las Vegas clubs. At the Dunes and at the single-deck tables at Caesar's Palace, the basic strategy player is at a .1 percent and .2 percent advantage, respectively, because of the favorable rules.

The use of two decks rather than a single deck costs the player .35 percent and the use of four decks, on the average, costs the player .51 percent. Thus, individual play at two-deck and four-deck games is not as advantageous to the player. Although some Vegas casinos that offer four-deck games are convinced that they have protected themselves from card counters, eventually more casinos may offer only six-deck games to further thwart the card-counting player.

TABLE 1

Effect of Rule Variations
on the Basic Strategy Player

Rule variations favorable to the player*		Effect on player's advantage
Double down on split pairs		+.13%
Surrender after first two cards		+.10
Drawing to split aces		+.14
2-to-1 payoff for blackjack		+2.32
Rule variations unfavorable to the player		
No doubling on:	Hard 11	−.89%
	Hard 10	−.56
	Hard 9	−.14
	Hard 8	0
	Soft hands	−.14
Dealer hits soft 17		−.20
Dealer takes no hole card		−.13
Two-deck (vs. single-deck)		−.35
Four-deck (vs. single-deck)		−.51
Tie hands won by dealer		−9.00

* The effect of these favorable rule variations on the card-counting player who is varying his bets is greater than stated here. For example, Braun states that surrender is worth +.25 percent to the player with a 1-to-4 bet variation.

TABLE 2

Average Expectation of Basic Strategy Player

	Northern Nevada	Downtown Las Vegas	Bahamas	Las Vegas Strip	Caesar's Palace*
Double down	On 10 and 11	On any two cards	On 9, 10, and 11	On any two cards	On any two cards and on split pairs
Dealer's soft 17	Hit	Hit	Stand	Stand	Stand
Split	Any pair	Any pair	Any pair	Any pair	Any pair
Single-deck	−.48%	−.20%	—	.00%	+.23%†
Two-deck	−.83	−.55	—	−.35	—
Four-deck	−.99	−.71	−.65%	−.51	−.28

* Caesar's Palace also offers a surrender option, whereby the player may throw in his hand after receiving two cards and lose only half his bet.
† Caesar's Palace offers single-deck at two to four tables in its casino, usually with $25 or $100 minimums; the rest of the games are four-deck and six-deck. The single-deck game is probably the most favorable legal game for the blackjack player in the world.

GLOSSaRY

Ace Adjustment: The running count adjusted for the number of aces remaining to be played.

Ace-poor Deck: A deck with a low proportion of aces remaining to be played. Favors the house.

Ace-rich Deck: A deck with a high proportion of aces remaining to be played. Favors the player.

Basic: A salary paid to counters who work for the team.

Basic Strategy: A system composed of the rules the player should follow in deciding whether to double down, split pairs, or take insurance. It allows the Las Vegas gambler to play blackjack about even with the house.

Black Chips: $100 chips.

Blackjack: Ace and a ten-valued card.

Burning: Removing the first card of a new deal and placing it in the discard pile or at the bottom of the deck.

Call-in Number: A prearranged count at which a counter signals in the Big Player to begin betting a hot deck.

Cold Deck: A deck unfavorable to the player.

Count: The numerical standing of the deck at any given time in play based on a set of preassigned values for each card denomination.

Counter: A person who uses a counting system such as Thorp or Revere to determine whether the deck is favorable or unfavorable to the player.

Cover: Measures used by the team to disguise their operation from casino personnel.

Double Down: A rule that allows the player to double the value of a bet after looking at his first two cards. He is then dealt one final card.

Element of Ruin: The team's calculation of the odds of losing their entire bank at a given betting level.

First Base: The far right-hand spot on the table.

Four-deck: A common Las Vegas blackjack game in which the house combines four decks and deals them from a plastic container known as a shoe.

Green Chips: $25 chips.

Hard 17:   Any combination of cards totaling 17 that does not include an eleven-valued ace.

Hit: A player's request for another card from the dealer.

Hole Card: The dealer's bottom card, which is dealt face down and not turned over until after players have played their hands.

Hot Deck: A deck highly favorable to the player. When a deck turns hot the counter signals in the B.P.

Insurance: A side bet that may equal half the player's original wager. If the dealer has blackjack the casino pays 2 to 1 on the insurance bet. If the dealer does not have blackjack he collects the insurance money. A bad bet for the noncounter.

Marker: A special casino check used by the gambler to draw more chips against his credit or money on deposit in the club cage.

Minus Count: A calculation indicating that a deck is favorable to the house.

Natural: A blackjack.

Pit: A section of the casino composed of several gaming tables.

Pit Boss: The casino official who supervises play at a group of gaming tables.

Plus Count: A calculation indicating that a deck is favorable to the player.

Running Count: Same as *count*.

Scam: Any method for bilking a gambling opponent.

Second Base: The middle spot on the table.

Shoe: A plastic container used to deal multiple-deck blackjack games.

Silver: Silver dollars or $1 gaming chips.

Single-deck: A blackjack game played with one deck.

Six-deck: A blackjack game played with six decks dealt from a shoe.

Sky: An area above the casino where officials observe play through one-way mirrors.

Split: A play in which the bettor may split two cards of identical value, betting an amount equal to his original wager on the second card.

Soft 17: A combination of cards totaling 17 that includes an ace valued as 11 (e.g., an ace and a 6).

Stand: A player's decision not to draw any additional cards.

Superhot Deck: A deck that exceeds the call-in number and is extremely favorable to the player.

Tapping out: Losing one's bank.

True Count: The running count adjusted for the number of decks or cards remaining to be played. Also called "the true."

Two-deck: A blackjack game played with two decks, usually dealt by hand.

Up-card: The dealer's card whose face is exposed to the player.

Warm Deck: A deck favorable to the player that is approaching the call-in number.